A tutorial introduction to occam 2

Dick Pountain
David May

March 11, 1988

A Tutorial Introduction to occam Programming

Dick Pountain
and David May

inmos®

BSP PROFESSIONAL BOOKS

OXFORD LONDON EDINBURGH

BOSTON PALO ALTO MELBOURNE

First published 1987 by
BSP Professional Books
8 John Street
London WC1N 2ES
A division of Blackwell Scientific Publications Ltd
Reprinted with amendments 1988

Printed and bound in Great Britain by Hollen St. Press,
Slough

British Library
Cataloguing in Publication Data

Pountain, Dick
   A tutorial introduction to occam programming.
   1. Occam (Computer program language)
   I. Title   II. May, David
   005.13'3   QA76.73.03

ISBN 0-632-01847-X

1	Introduction	3
2	Signposts	5
3	The concepts	7
4	Fundamentals of occam	15
5	Arrays in occam	41
6	Channel communication	47
7	Characters and strings	53
8	Replicators	57
9	Real-time programming in occam	69
10	Configuration	73
11	Terminating concurrent programs	79
12	Occam programming style	83
13	Occam 2 language definition	91
	13.1 Introduction	91
	13.2 Notation	91
	13.3 Process	92
	13.4 Replicator	95
	13.5 Multiple assignment	96
	13.6 Types	96
	13.7 Scope	98
	13.8 Protocol	100
	13.9 Procedure	102
	13.10 Variable, Channel and Timer	102
	13.11 Literal	103
	13.12 Expression	104
	13.13 Function	107
	13.14 Timer input	108
	13.15 Character set	109
	13.16 Configuration	110
	13.17 Invalid processes	110
	13.18 Retyping	111
	13.19 External input and output	111
	13.20 Usage rules check list	112

1 Introduction

The aim of this tutorial is to introduce the reader to concurrent programming using the occam language. It will provide examples of occam programs, and discuss the novel concepts which occam employs. It is not however the definitive guide to the syntax of occam; that you will find in the Formal Definition by David May which forms the second half of this book.

occam is rapidly being recognised as a solution to the problem of programming concurrent systems of all kinds, and as a powerful and expressive calculus for describing concurrent algorithms.

occam bears a special relationship with the INMOS Transputer, a high performance single chip computer whose architecture facilitates the construction of parallel processing systems. The Transputer executes occam programs more or less directly (i.e. occam is the "assembly language of the Transputer").

Parallel computer systems can be designed in occam, and then implemented using Transputers as "hardware occam processes". This intimate relation between the software and hardware will be novel to most system designers, who are perhaps used to a more rigid division of labour.

The approach taken in this manual is therefore governed by the realisation that some of its potential readers will not be professional programmers, but rather professional engineers and system designers who wish to use occam to design hardware systems.

For this reason we do not assume extensive knowledge of any other high-level computer language, nor of machine level programming, on the part of the reader. We do however assume a familiarity with the general concepts of computing and computer programming; it is not a manual for the novice to computing.

The tutorial is concerned purely with the language occam and will only briefly address the issues of installing occam programs onto Transputer systems. It is intended as a general introduction to the language, equally suitable for those readers who intend to use occam on conventional computers.

We shall not insist that any particular computer/compiler combination (or indeed any hardware at all) be available to the reader; hardware dependent aspects of occam are concentrated into a single chapter at the end of the course.

For the same reasons, there will be no instruction in the detailed workings of particular occam compilers. Error reporting will not be covered except in a general way. Details of this kind are to be found in the manual which accompanies an occam compiler.

Acknowledgements: Many thanks to the INMOS staff who took time out from writing the compiler and other things to check this text and to improve the examples. In particular my thanks to David May, Ron Laborde and Steven Ericsson Zenith. Steven has kept this book up to date during the course of the language development which took place during 1986 and 1987.

2 Signposts

As an aid to the reader, the author has placed a variety of signposts throughout the text, to signal points of special interest. The meaning of these signposts is as follows.

Take care: Sections so marked are those which explain concepts which are especially likely to trip up novice occam programmers. This may be because:

1 This concept is intrinsically difficult.

2 occam handles this area in a different way from traditional languages with which the reader may be familiar.

3 This is a limitation or restriction in current implementations of occam.

These sections will repay frequent re-reading, especially if you have written an occam program that doesn't work!

Hint: These are tricks and devices which proved useful to the author while learning occam.

Key Idea: A concept which is fundamental to the understanding of occam. Make sure you thoroughly grasp it.

Aside: A brief digression from the main thread of the tutorial into broader computing matters. Experienced programmers might wish to skip them.

Technical Note: A brief explanation of some implementation issue. If you don't understand it, don't let it hold you up but skip it and return later.

3 The concepts

Concurrency

Since John Von Neumann discovered the principles over 40 years ago, all digital computers have been designed in a fundamentally similar way.

A processor, which can perform a set of basic numeric manipulations, is connected to a memory system which can store numbers. Some of these numbers are the data which the computer is required to process. The other numbers are instructions to the processor and tell it which of its basic manipulations to perform.

The instructions are passed to the processor one after the other, and executed. Execution of a computer program is sequential, consisting of a series of primitive actions following one another in time.

Everyday examples of similar activities in the real world could be reading a book (one word at a time), or "executing" a knitting pattern by following the instructions in sequence.

Computers are mainly employed to model the real world. Even the simple act of adding 2 and 2 is a model of the real world, except when it is performed by or for a mathematician who is interested in the pure properties of numbers. Far more frequently 2+2 is a model for the act of adding two pounds, or dollars, or apples, or airplanes, to an existing stock of two.

Certainly the major applications of computers, such as accounting, banking, weather forecasting, process control and even word processing, are explicitly modelling objects, events and activities in the real world.

The world which we inhabit is inherently concurrent. At the scale of human affairs, indeed at any scale between the cosmological and the quantum mechanical, the world behaves as if it were organised into three spatial dimensions and one time dimension.

Events happen in both time and space. It is possible for two events to occur in the same place one after the other in time (i.e. sequentially), and equally possible for events to occur in different places at the same time (i.e. concurrently, or in parallel).

Concurrency is so much a feature of the universe that we are not normally concerned with it at all. The fact that, for instance, the population of this planet all live different lives in different places at the present time is so obvious that one feels slightly embarrassed in stating it.

However it is worthwhile to reflect on the contrast between the concurrent nature of the world, and the sequential nature of the digital computer. Since the main purpose of the computer is to model the world, there would seem to be a serious mismatch.

In order to model the world with a computer, programmers of conventional computers have to find ways to mimic concurrent events using a sequence of instructions. This is not a problem in an application like accounting, where it is perfectly reasonable to regard goods despatched, materials and moneys flowing in and out as happening sequentially in time.

It is more of a problem when you wish to control a petro-chemicals plant by computer. Every process in every part of the plant must be monitored and controlled at the same time, all the time. It is not acceptable for a crisis in one reaction vessel to be overlooked because the computer happened to be looking at a different reactor at the time.

Concurrent programming

The earliest digital computers were programmed using the basic numeric instructions understood by the processor. Such programming is so tedious and error prone that computer scientists soon began to design "high-level" languages, starting with Fortran and leading to the current proliferation which includes Basic, Pascal, Modula 2, C, Ada, Forth, Lisp, Prolog and hundreds of others.

These languages allow programmers to express the logic of a program in notations which use readable

English (or French etc...) words, albeit with a tightly constrained and reduced syntax. A program called a compiler then translates these notations into the basic numeric instructions which the computer understands.

For the majority of languages, the product of the compiler is again a sequence of instructions, to be executed one at a time by the processor just as if they had been produced by hand. In other words these languages faithfully reflect the nature of the underlying sequential Von Neumann computer in a form more palatable to human programmers.

To adequately model the concurrency of the real world, it would be preferable to have many processors all working at the same time on the same program. There are also huge potential performance benefits to be derived from such parallel processing. For regardless of how far electronic engineers can push the speed of an individual processor, ten of them running concurrently will still execute ten times as many instructions in a second.

Conventional programming languages are not well equipped to construct programs for such multiple processors as their very design assumes the sequential execution of instructions.

Some languages have been modified to allow concurrent programs to be written, but the burden of ensuring that concurrent parts of the program are synchronised (i.e. that they cooperate rather than fight) is placed on the programmer. This leads to such programming being perceived as very much more difficult than ordinary sequential programming.

occam is the first language to be based upon the concept of parallel, in addition to sequential, execution, and to provide automatic communication and synchronisation between concurrent processes.

Synchronisation

It's possible to write concurrent programs in conventional programming languages, and to run them on conventional computers; in essence what happens is that the programmer writes a number of programs and the computer pretends to run them all at the same time by running a piece of each one in turn, swapping at very short intervals, until they are all done.

However, this kind of programming is more difficult than straightforward "do this, then do this, then do this" sequential programming. Crudely put, this is because a sequential program has only one beginning and one end, but a concurrent program may have many beginnings and many ends.

A sequential program starts, runs and then finishes; it's either running or it's not. Often we are not even concerned about exactly when it finishes (though we usually want it to be as quick as possible on a given computer).

The well worn metaphor of a knitting pattern can be instructive here. A knitting pattern consists of a list of instructions on how to manipulate wool and needles, which if followed faithfully lead to the production of, say, a sweater.

Some instructions will have to be repeated many times, and the pattern will use an appropriate notation which tells the knitter to do this without having to write out every single step, just like the repetition structures of computer languages.

For a single knitter who isn't in a hurry, the sweater will take as long as it takes to knit; the sweater is finished when they've performed every instruction in the pattern.
In occam this could be represented by, say:

```
SEQ
   ...knit body
   ...knit sleeve
   ...knit sleeve
   ...knit neck
```

where the SEQ means "do all these in sequence".

Aside: The convention of using of three dots . . . will be used throughout the rest of this tutorial to describe parts of a program, in ordinary English, whose internal details are not relevant to the example, as with ...`knit body`. They should be distinguished from pure comments, introduced by two dashes, as in --`This is a Comment`. Such comments are purely for explanation purposes and do not form part of the program.

But what about a small firm of knitters, who split up the sweaters into components (bodies, necks, sleeves) and share out the jobs? They have orders to fulfill and so time now matters.

The most efficient way to proceed is for everyone to knit their individual bits concurrently. Unfortunately the finishers who put sweaters together can't make a sweater until they have a neck, two sleeves and a body....

From a picture of unconcerned rural bliss by the fireside we switch to one of irascible finishers screaming "hurry up with that sleeve". The point being that finishing the pattern for a sleeve is no longer sufficient indication that the sweater is finished.

The time of finishing now matters very much and, more importantly, finishing one job may depend on the finishing of other jobs outside the individual knitter's control. Unless all the knitters' activities can be suitably synchronised the result is very inefficient production, with everyone waiting on the slowest knitter.

Computers magnify this problem enormously. They are not as intelligent nor as patient as even the most bad tempered of knitters. If several cooperating programs don't finish their parts of the job at the right times, the result is usually that the program won't run at all, rather than it merely running inefficiently.

Computers are infinitely patient in another sense, for a program is perfectly prepared to wait forever for something which will never arrive because the synchronisation is wrong (a situation known to concurrent programmers as *deadlock*).

This being so, concurrent programs can be difficult to write. Achieving the necessary synchronisation between parts has up until now been largely the responsibility of the programmer, who has to write in an elaborate system of signals by which each part can tell the others whether or not it is ready.

Each part of the program must continually look at these signals to see whether or not it can carry on. The program code required to achieve this is often considerable, and writing it consumes a lot of time which the programmer could have spent writing those parts of the program which actually do the job (knitting sweaters so to speak).

Given a concurrent program of any complexity it becomes difficult for the programmer to even understand how the parts should relate at all.

occam simplifies the writing of concurrent programs by taking most of the burden of synchronisation away from the programmer. For instance, our concurrent knitters could be described by:

```
SEQ
  PAR
    ...knit body
    ...knit left sleeve
    ...knit right sleeve
    ...knit neck
  ...sew sweater
```

This expresses the fact that the parts are knitted in parallel (**PAR**) but that sewing follows sequentially when all the parts are finished.

Communication between the different parts of a program is built into the language itself, and it is synchronised communication - that is, a message will only be sent when both the sender and the receiver are ready.

If one party becomes ready before the other, it will automatically wait for the other without any explicit command from the programmer. The only responsibility left with the programmer is that of avoiding deadlock by ensuring that the second party becomes ready sometime (that someone actually is knitting that sleeve!).

We could add such communications to our knitting description like this:

```
PAR
  SEQ                              -- body
    ...knit body                   -- knitter
    ...output body
  SEQ
    ...knit right sleeve           -- sleeve
    ...output right sleeve         -- knitter
    ...knit left sleeve
    ...output left sleeve
  SEQ                              -- neck
    ...knit neck                   -- knitter
    ...output neck
  SEQ                              -- finisher
    PAR
      ...input body
      SEQ
        ...input right sleeve
        ...input left sleeve
      ...input neck
    ...sew sweater
```

This is a description of the making of one sweater by four knitters all working at the same time, and all the synchronisation required is implied in its structure. It works by combining simple processes ("knit body") into larger processes (each kind of knitter) which can themselves be combined into a still larger process (make a sweater).

Processes and channels

In occam programming we refer to the parts of a program as processes.

Key Idea: A process starts, performs a number of actions and then finishes.

This definition fits an ordinary sequential program, but in occam more than one process may be executing at the same time, and processes can send messages to one another.

In conventional programming languages such as BASIC, much of the activity of a program consists of changing the values, such as numbers or strings of characters, stored in variables. Take for example this rather unexciting BASIC program:

```
10 LET A = 2
20 LET B = A
40 PRINT B
50 END
```

The result of running this program is that the value in both variables **A** and **B** becomes **2**, and line 40 causes this value to be printed out on a VDU screen.

There is communication of a limited sort going on in this program. The **PRINT** command provides one-way communication between the program and an external device, the VDU screen.

There is also a sense in which the value **2** has been communicated from **A** to **B**, though we wouldn't normally dignify this act with the name "communication" because there is only one BASIC program running and it's being executed one line after another. Instead we tend to regard the value **2** as being stored in both **A** and **B**.

Now imagine that we could have two such programs running at the same time on different computers and that in some as yet unspecified way they can communicate across space:

```
10 LET A = 2                          10 LET B = A
20 END                                20 END
```
            computer 1   computer 2

The desired result is that the value of **A** somehow crosses the gap between the computers and sets **B** to 2.

It is of course possible to achieve this end with a BASIC program; one could for instance connect the computers together by means of serial communication ports. But the BASIC programs would both need to have extra lines added containing special input and output instructions to send or receive data from the serial port, and to match the physical attributes of the ports (e.g. bits/second and word length), something like:

```
10 LET A = 2                          10 RSCONFIG ..
20 RSCONFIG ..                        20 RSINPUT A
30 RSOUTPUT A                         20 LET B = A
40 END                                40 END
```
            computer 1   computer 2

occam permits this sort of communication as a normal feature of programming, and doesn't require special instructions which have to be different for each kind of communications device.

More importantly, occam doesn't mind whether the two programs which so communicate are running on different computers, or are just two processes running concurrently on the same computer.

As well as variables for storing values, occam uses channels for communicating values. Channels look in many ways like variables, except that rather than assigning a value to them for storage (e.g. **LET A = 2** in BASIC) we output to them or input from them.

The value output by one process is input by another process, the channel behaving like a pipe joining the two processes. A single channel can only join two processes; it's like a person-to-person call rather than a conference. Channels are one-way only, so two would be needed for a two way communication.

Key Idea: A channel is a one-way, point-to-point link from one process to one other process.

A transfer over a channel is actually an act of copying; if the value is output from a variable, then that variable retains its value and a copy of it is sent over the channel.

occam uses the symbol **!** to mean output and **?** to mean input so we could express the above examples by:

```
A ! 2                                 A ? B
```
            process 1   process 2

where **A** is a channel and **B** is a variable. This reads as "output 2 to **A**" and "input from **A** to **B**".

Since processes 1 and 2 are independent, they might well be executed at different times. The act of transferring a value from one end of the channel to the other can only happen when both processes are ready.

In other words, if the output in process 1 is executed before the input in process 2 executes, process 1 will automatically wait for process 2 before sending a value. Vice versa, if the input in process 2 were executed before process 1 had output, process 2 would wait for a value to appear. There is no way for a value to be output into "thin air" and lost.

With our hypothetical BASIC programs above there is no such assurance. What would happen should the programs be "out of step" depends on the detailed workings of the particular link we used.

It might well be that if program 1 reached **RSOUTPUT A** before program 2 reached **RSINPUT A**, the value of **A** would be sent and lost. Equally if program 2 arrived first it might stop the program and report an error such as "bad connection".

The two novel features which distinguish channels from variables are:

1) A channel can pass values either between two processes running on the same computer, or between two processes running on different computers. In the first case the channel would in fact be just a location in memory, rather like a variable. In the second case the channel could represent a real hardware link, such as a Transputer link or other serial communication line. Both cases are represented identically in an occam program.

Key Idea: An occam channel describes communication in the abstract, and does not depend upon its physical implementation. You can thus write and test a program using channels without having to worry about exactly where the different processes will be executed. The program can be developed on a single processor workstation; when it's finished and proved you may decide to distribute various processes in the program onto different computers, and do so by making a few simple declarations at the beginning of the program.

2) Channels are patient and polite. If an input process finds that no value is ready it will wait until one is supplied, without any explicit instruction from the programmer. Equally an output will not send until the receiver is ready. This introduces the time factor into programming, but in a way which lifts much of the responsibility for "timekeeping" off the programmers shoulders.

The description of our knitters could now be written using channels to transport the parts:

```
PAR
  SEQ                          -- body knitter
    ...knit body
    bodychan ! body
  SEQ                          -- sleeve knitter
    ...knit right sleeve
    sleevechan ! right.sleeve
    ...knit left sleeve
    sleevechan ! left.sleeve
  SEQ                          -- neck knitter
    ...knit neck
    neckchan ! neck
  SEQ                          -- finisher
    PAR
      bodychan ? body
      SEQ
        sleevechan ? right.sleeve
        sleevechan ? left.sleeve
      neckchan ? neck
    ...sew sweater
```

Three different channels are needed because each may only join two processes; for example bodychan joins the body knitter to the finisher. As we shall see in the next chapter, when occam is used as a computer language, rather than for an informal description as here, channels and variables must be declared before they are used.

Communication over self-synchronising channels is a novel and powerful part of occam, and it can render the writing of concurrent programs a far less formidable task than it is with conventional languages. In the next chapter we shall start in earnest to construct occam programs from the simple processes just outlined.

4 Fundamentals of occam

Primitive processes

All occam programs are built from combinations of three kinds of primitive process. We have seen all three kinds already; they are assignment, input and output.

Assignment process

An assignment process changes the value of a variable, just as it would in most conventional languages. The symbol for assignment in occam is `:=`. So the assignment process:

```
fred := 2
```

makes the value in variable **fred** two. The value assigned to a variable could be an expression such as:

```
fred := 2 + 5
```

and this expression could contain other variables:

```
fred := 5 - jim
```

Take care: Be sure not to mix up = and :=. In occam = means a test for equality, not an assignment.

Multiple assignment, assignment to more than one variable at the same time, is also possible in occam:

```
fred, john := 2, 3
```

This multiple assignment process makes the value in the variable **fred** two, and the value in the variable **john** three. This is really useful for swapping the value of variables:

```
fred, john := john, fred
```

It is important to note however, that the rules of occam do not allow a variable to appear more than once on the left side of a multiple assignment. So:

```
fred, fred := 2, 3    -- ILLEGAL! same variable twice on the left
```

Aside: This is not a particularly useful thing to do anyway, but it is important to realise when using variables in the subscript of an array, as we shall see later.

Input process

An input process inputs a value from a channel into a variable. The symbol for input in occam is `?`. The input process:

```
chan3 ? fred
```

takes a value from a channel called **chan3** and puts it into variable **fred**.

Input processes can only input values to variables. It is quite meaningless to input to a constant or to an expression.

An input process cannot proceed until a corresponding output process on the same channel is ready.

Hint: As an aid to memory think of the question mark as meaning "Where's my value ?"

Output process

An output process outputs a value to a channel. The symbol for output in occam is **!**. The output process:

```
chan3 ! 2
```

outputs the value **2** to a channel called **chan3**.

The value output to a channel can be anything that you could assign to a variable, so it may be a variable or an expression, and the expression may contain variables.

An output process cannot proceed until a corresponding input process on the same channel is ready.

Hint: As an aid to memory, think of the exclamation mark as meaning "Here's your value !".

Communication

Communication over a channel can only occur when both input and output processes are ready. If during the execution of a program, an input process is reached before its corresponding output process is reached, the input will wait until the output becomes ready. Should the output be reached first, it will wait for its input.

A value communicated over a channel is copied to the input variable and the value of the output variable remains unchanged.

Key Idea: Communication is synchronised.

These then are the building blocks from which occam programs are made. Each such primitive process must occupy a separate line in an occam program, and is the simplest action that occam can perform, an "atom" of occam programming.

Key Idea: occam programs are built by combining primitive processes.

SKIP and STOP

occam has two special processes called **SKIP** and **STOP**.

Key Idea: The process **SKIP** starts, does nothing and then finishes.

SKIP may be thought of as representing a process which does nothing. It might be used in a partly completed program in place of a process which will be written later, but which for the moment can be allowed to do nothing.

For example a process which is to drive an electric motor could be replaced by **SKIP** when testing the program without a motor. There are also occasions when you want nothing to happen, but the syntax of occam requires a process to be present.

Key Idea: The process **STOP** starts but never proceeds and never finishes.

STOP may be thought of as representing a process which doesn't work, or is "broken". It might be used, like **SKIP**, to stand in for a process which has yet to be written.

For example a process to handle errors could be replaced by **STOP** in the early stages of testing a program.

The effect of a "broken" process tends to spread, because any process which communicates with a broken process will itself never finish, and hence it becomes broken too.

Termination and stopping

So far we have loosely used the term "finish" when referring to processes. Concurrent programming in occam requires us to be rather more precise than this.

A process which completes all its actions is said to terminate. Normally a process starts, proceeds and then terminates.

A process which cannot proceed is said to be stopped which is not at all the same thing. A stopped program never terminates. A process might be stopped by waiting for an event which will never happen, due to a programming error, in which case it is said to be deadlocked.

Correct termination of concurrent programs is not a trivial matter, since they may have many parallel processes which communicate with one another. This topic is of sufficient importance to merit a chapter to itself (see Chapter 9).

Constructions

Several primitive processes can be combined into a larger process by specifying that they should be performed one after the other, or all at the same time. This larger process is called a construction and it begins with an occam keyword which states how the component processes are to be combined.

SEQ construction

The simplest construction to understand is the **SEQ** (pronounce it "seek"), short for sequence, which merely says "do the following processes one after another". Here is an example:

```
SEQ
  chan3 ? fred
  jim := fred + 1
  chan4 ! jim
```

This says, "do in sequence, input from **chan3** to **fred**, assign **fred + 1** to **jim** and output **jim** to **chan4**". In sequence means, to be more precise, that the next process does not start until the previous one has terminated. A **SEQ** process therefore works just like a program in any conventional programming language; it finishes when its last component process finishes.

Notice the way that the processes which make up this **SEQ** process are indented by two characters from the word **SEQ**, so that they line up under the Q. This is not merely to make the program look prettier, but is the way that occam knows which processes are part of the **SEQ**.

Whenever a construction is built, we indicate the extent of the new process by indenting all its component processes by two characters. Other languages use special characters like { . . . } or **begin . . . end** for this purpose, but occam uses indentation alone.

Key Idea: A **SEQ** construction terminates when its last process terminates.

Take care: **SEQ** is compulsory in occam whenever two or more processes are to run in sequence. In conventional programming languages, sequence is taken for granted and merely writing one statement after another guarantees they will execute in sequence. Because occam offers other modes of execution apart from the sequential, sequence must be explicitly requested.

PAR construction

The **PAR** construction, short for parallel, says "do the following processes all at the same time", i.e. in parallel. All the component processes of a **PAR** start to execute simultaneously. For example:

```
PAR
  SEQ
    chan3 ? fred
    fred := fred + 1
  SEQ
    chan4 ? jim
    jim := jim + 1
```

says "at the same time, input from **chan3** to **fred** and then add one to the result, whilst receiving input from **chan4** to **jim** and then adding one to the result".

Notice again the indentation. The first two character indent tells occam that the **PAR** process consists of two **SEQ** processes. The second level of indentation shows that each **SEQ** is composed of two primitive processes.

Notice also that the processes which are to run in parallel are still written in sequence just as in any ordinary program. This is purely a matter of writing convenience. The designers of occam could have chosen to make us write parallel processes side by side, which would give a stronger impression of what is going on:

```
PAR
  SEQ                        SEQ
    chan3 ? fred               chan4 ? jim
    fred := fred + 1           jim := jim + 1
```

As you will quickly see though, this would become hopelessly clumsy once you had more than two or three parallel processes in a **PAR**; it would exceed the width of standard VDU screens and printer paper, as well as involving the typist in tedious tabulation.

The important thing to keep in mind is that in a **PAR**, the written order of the component processes is irrelevant as they are all performed at the same time. **PAR** is not quite so easy to understand as **SEQ**, because the idea of things happening simultaneously in computer programs is new to many programmers.

For instance we can now no longer know for sure which of the two parallel processes in the above example will finish first ; it depends upon which input becomes ready first, which in turn depends upon a couple of output processes elsewhere in the program.

The beauty of occam is that this doesn't matter, because the **PAR** construction itself has a single well defined beginning and a single well defined end. We know that the two **SEQ** processes will start at the same time, run when their inputs become ready and then terminate.

All the component processes in a **PAR** start at the same time, and the **PAR** itself terminates when all its component processes have terminated and that is all we need to know.

Key Idea: This is the central principle of occam programming; compound processes built up from simpler processes behave just like simple processes i.e. they start, perform actions and then terminate. They can in turn become the components of a still more complex process.

There is a lot more to be said about **PAR**, especially in relation to communication over channels. Moreover there are several more constructions in occam, which build processes that repeat or make conditional choices.

But before going on to such matters, something needs to be clarified. Up till now we have been using channels and variables like **chan3** and **fred** as if they, so to speak, grew on trees. This is most definitely not the case; in occam both channels and variables need to be specified before they can be used. It makes sense to discuss specifications and types before we go any further, so that the examples we study can be valid occam programs.

Types, specifications and scope

occam, like Pascal and many other languages, but unlike BASIC, requires that every object that is used by a program should have a type which tells occam what sort of object it is dealing with. Furthermore the type of an object must be specified before it can be used in a process.

We have been using named channels (**chan3** and **chan4**) and variables (**fred** and **jim**) without any specification so far, a situation which will now be rectified.

Names

First let's deal with names themselves. In occam the names of objects can be as long as you like, and they must start with a letter of the alphabet. The rest of the name, if there is one, can be made up of letters, digits and the dot character. Upper and lower case are distinguished by occam, so that **fred** and **Fred** are different names. These are all valid names:

        x Y fred chan3 Chan3 new.fred old.fred

occam keywords such as **SEQ**, **PAR** and **CHAN** are always in upper case and they are reserved. In other words they cannot be used as names that you create.

These are not valid names:

```
        3chan      -- doesn't start with a letter
        old-fred -- contains illegal character '-'
        fred$      -- contains illegal character '$'
        old fred -- contains a space
        CHAN       -- reserved word CHAN
```

Data types

Variables may take on one of several data types, i.e. kinds of value. The following are the types which are always provided by occam:

```
        INT     -- an integer or whole number.
        BYTE    -- an integer between 0 and 255;
                -- very often used to
                -- represent characters.
        BOOL    -- one of the logical truth
                -- values TRUE or FALSE.
```

We could specify the variables in the above examples as:

        INT fred, jim :

which means that they can be used to represent positive or negative whole numbers. Several variables may be specified at once, as above, by listing them separated by commas.

Technical Note: occam actually provides more data types than those outlined above. Catering for non-integral numbers by supplying various Real Number types. These types also provide fixed length number representation. **INT16**, **INT32**, **INT64**, **REAL32**, **REAL64** are numeric types represented using 16, 32 or 64 bits respectively. The details of these types can be studied in the Formal Definition at the rear of this book. For the purposes of this tutorial we will work only with **INT**, **BYTE** and **BOOL** and will make no assumptions about the physical size of an **INT**.

Channel type and protocol

Channels are all of the type **CHAN OF** *protocol*. It is necessary to specify the data type and structure of the values that they are to carry. This is called the channel protocol. For the present we shall be content to regard channels as able to carry single values of a single data type, rather like variables.

A channel which carries single integer values would be specified by:

```
CHAN OF INT chan3 :
```

where the **INT** specifies the type of values which may pass along the channel **chan3**. The type of **chan3** is **CHAN OF INT**. In general the protocol of a channel is specified by **CHAN OF** *protocol*.

Timer type

The type **TIMER** allows the creation of timers which can be used as clocks by processes. Timers will be discussed further in Chapter 7.

Characters and strings

occam does not have any type **CHAR** or **STRING** to represent alphabetic characters or words. Instead characters are represented as numbers of type **BYTE** and strings as arrays of numbers of type **BYTE**. We shall return to this subject in a later chapter.

Boolean type

Boolean values, or truth values are produced as the result of tests performed by comparison operators. occam provides the following tests:

```
=       -- equal to
<>      -- not equal to
>       -- greater than
<       -- less than
>=      -- greater than or equal to
<=      -- less than or equal to
```

These tests may only be applied to two values of the same type, and they always yield a value of type **BOOL**. For example the test 2 **<>** 3 yields the value **TRUE** since 2 does not equal 3.

The truth values **TRUE** and **FALSE** are occam constants which can be used in any situation where a test could be used; you may like to think of them as tests whose outcome is decided in advance.

Constants

A name can be given to a constant value by specifying it with:

VAL *type name* **IS** *value*:

So we could write:

```
VAL INT year IS 365:
VAL INT leap.year IS 366:
```

The type can be omitted as occam can deduce it from the value:

> **VAL year IS 365:**

Possible ambiguities over **BYTE** and **INT** are resolved by explicitly specifying the type of the value, which we'll see later on.

Notice the colon, which is used to end all the different kinds of specification. This colon joins a specification to the process which follows it.

Scope

In occam, variables, channels and other named objects are local to the process which immediately follows their specification. What this means is that the object to which the name refers effectively does not exist inside any other process. For instance in this example:

```
PAR
  INT fred :
  SEQ
    chan3 ? fred
    ...more processes
  INT jim :
  SEQ
    chan4 ? fred
    ...more processes
```

an error will be reported, because **fred** exists only inside the first **SEQ** and **jim** exists only inside the second **SEQ**. The second **fred** will therefore look to occam like an unspecified variable.

The colon which ends a specification in effect joins the specification to the process which follows it and, to reinforce the connection, specifications are indented to the same level as the process. This following process is the scope throughout which the specification holds.

The same name may be used for different objects with different scopes. For instance, we could use **fred** for both variables in the above example:

```
PAR
  INT fred :
  SEQ
    chan3 ? fred
    ...more processes
  INT fred :
  SEQ
    chan4 ? fred
    ...more processes
```

the two **fred**s are now different variables, each local to its own **SEQ** process, and altering the value of **fred** in the first process has no effect on the second.

If inside the scope of a variable (or other named object), another variable is specified with the same name, then within its own scope this namesake replaces the original. The original object is masked by the newcomer.

For example:

```
INT fred :
SEQ
  chan3 ? fred
  INT fred :
  SEQ
    chan4 ? fred
    ...more processes
  ...more processes
```

In this case, the input from **chan4** goes into the second **fred**, and the first **fred** is effectively invisible throughout the second, nested **SEQ**. Let's now fix up the **PAR** example we saw in an earlier section with some correct declarations:

```
CHAN OF INT chan3, chan4:
PAR
  INT fred:
  SEQ
    chan3 ? fred
    fred := fred + 1
  INT jim:
  SEQ
    chan4 ? jim
    jim := jim + 1
```

Now the channels **chan3** and **chan4** are known throughout the **PAR** process; we could legally refer to either of them in either of the **SEQ**s. On the other hand **fred** and **jim** are known only within their respective **SEQ**s.

Take care: Specifying a variable in occam does not initialise its value to zero. The value of a variable is undefined garbage until it has been assigned to or has input a value. The value of a variable only has meaning during the execution of the process for which it is declared. Since the variable doesn't exist outside this process, it makes no sense to ask what is its value outside the process. But more importantly, it makes no sense either to ask what is its value once the process has terminated. The next time that process is executed, the variable starts out as undefined garbage again. You cannot and must not assume that it keeps the value which it had at the end of the previous execution. For example:

```
WHILE x >= 0   --ILLEGAL! x not declared here
  INT x :
  SEQ
    input ? x
    output ! x

INT x :
WHILE x >= 0   -- unwise: x is garbage here
  SEQ
    input ? x
    output ! x

INT x :
SEQ
  x := 0
  WHILE x >= 0      -- correct
    SEQ
      input ? x
      output ! x
```

(**WHILE** is one way that occam uses to repeatedly execute a process; we'll see it in more detail soon).

Hint: If you need a variable to keep its value from one execution of a process to another, declare it in an outer scope that is, before a process which contains the process which is being repeatedly executed.

Communicating processes

Communication between parallel processes is the essence of occam programming.

At its simplest it requires two processes executing in parallel and a channel joining them:

```
INT x :
CHAN OF INT comm :
PAR
   comm ! 2
   comm ? x
```

This trivial program merely outputs the value 2 from one process and inputs it into the variable **x** in the second. Its overall effect is exactly as if we had a single process which assigned 2 to **x**.

Shared variables : a warning

Communication between the component processes of a **PAR** must only be done using channels. occam doesn't allow us to pass values between parallel processes by using a shared variable.

In fact if a component of a **PAR** contains an assignment or input to a variable, then the variable must not be used at all in any other component:

```
INT x, y :
PAR
   SEQ
      x := 2
      ... more processes
   SEQ
      y := x        -- ILLEGAL!
      ... more processes
```

Keeping variables local to component processes and using channels to communicate values is the right way to do it.

This may seem like a severe restriction to programmers who have experience with conventional languages. It will certainly be the biggest source of errors when first programming in occam.

Like all prohibitions it will be more easily borne if the reason for it is understood. The reason is both simple and necessary.

Parallel processes run at the same time, and in general they run asynchronously i.e. at their own pace, only coming into synchronisation with each other briefly when forced to by communication over a channel.

If occam allowed one parallel process to read from a variable which has its value altered in another parallel process, what value will be read? It depends upon whether or not the other process has altered it yet, and this can't be known since the processes are asynchronous. And what if the altering process chooses to alter the variable's value at the precise moment that the second process is reading it? What would the value be then?

Such a scheme is obviously unworkable, hence the prohibition. But couldn't we organise it so that a variable warns the other process that it has had its value changed? We could indeed; the resulting object already exists in occam and is called a channel! Q.E.D.

Key Idea: In occam variables are used for storing values, while channels are used for communicating values.

Let's now return to the main track with a more complicated example of a **PAR** which performs some arithmetic on a value before passing it on:

```
CHAN OF INT comm:
PAR
  INT x:
  SEQ
    input ? x
    comm ! 2 * x
  INT y:
  SEQ
    comm ? y
    output ! y + 1
```

Here we have two channels called **input** and **output** which lead to other processes or perhaps to the outside world. We assume that they have been declared elsewhere in a larger program. This piece of program uses two processes working in parallel one of which multiplies an input value by two, the other adds one to the result and sends it on its way to the output. The times-two process and the add-one process communicate on channel **comm**.

Aside: In case it worries you, this is not a particularly useful thing to do; it is purely for illustration. It would be much simpler to do times-two and add-one in a single **SEQ** process, or indeed in a single expression. But later on when we have more of occam at our disposal, we shall see how this sort of thing can be very useful indeed. At this early stage, all examples of communicating **PAR**s will tend unfortunately to appear trivial.

It's been said several times already that an occam channel is a one-way link between a pair of processes, but it is useful to now examine exactly what this implies. In a communicating PAR construct it means that:

1) Only two component processes of the **PAR** may use any particular channel, one as the sender and the other as receiver.

```
CHAN OF INT comm:
PAR
  SEQ
    comm ! 2
  INT y:
  SEQ
    comm ? y
  INT z:        -- ILLEGAL! two processes
  SEQ           -- inputting from same channel
    comm ? z
```

2) The sender process must only contain outputs to the channel and the receiver must only contain inputs from the channel.

```
CHAN OF INT comm:
PAR
  SEQ
    comm ! 2
  INT y:
  SEQ
    comm ? y
    comm ! y+1
    -- ILLEGAL! input and output
    -- from the same channel in
    -- the same process
```

For two-way communication between two processes we would need two channels:

```
CHAN OF INT comm1, comm2:
PAR
  INT x:
  SEQ
    comm1 ! 2
    comm2 ? x
  INT y:
  SEQ
    comm1 ? y
    comm2 ! 3
```

The effect is that each process sends a value to the other; **x** ends up with the value **3** and **y** with the value **2**. The order of the inputs and outputs in each **SEQ** matters very much here and it's important to understand why.

If we were to write:

```
CHAN OF INT comm1, comm2:
PAR
  INT x:
  SEQ
    comm2 ? x
    comm1 ! 2
  INT y:
  SEQ
    comm1 ? y
    comm2 ! 3
```

then the program would never terminate; we have the dreaded deadlock.

Why deadlock? Because both **SEQ**s wait patiently for an input to become ready. But since each is waiting for the other to output, neither can proceed to make the necessary output! It's rather like those comical scenes when two people passing in a narrow doorway repeatedly step to the same side to make way, so repeatedly blocking each other. Swapping the input and output in either process resolves the deadlock.

Take care: Sequence your programs to ensure that two parallel processes are never each waiting for a sequentially later output from the other. This is the only circumstance in which occam requires you to worry about such matters, but watch out for it. Like certain stalemates in the game of chess, it may be disguised in complex processes.

Repetitive processes

All programming languages provide some means of looping, i.e. performing an action repeatedly. In general it's convenient to distinguish two kinds of repetition; repeat for a specified number of times, or repeat while a given condition holds. occam has both types of repetition. The first, or counted loop we'll see later on. The second conditional loop is performed by a construction called **WHILE**, which includes a test such as **x < 0** or **fred = 100**. The resulting process is executed while the test result is true, or looked at another way, until it becomes false.

For example:

```
INT x :
SEQ
  x := 0
  WHILE x >= 0
    SEQ
      input ? x
      output ! x
```

will continue to read values from channel **input** and send them to **output** so long as the value is not less than zero. Every time the inner **SEQ** process terminates, the **WHILE** process will be performed again and the test repeated. This continues so long as the test result is **TRUE** i.e. so long as **x** is greater than or equal to zero. When a negative value is received the **WHILE** process terminates.

Aside: The net effect of this process is to buffer (i.e. store) a single value on its way from input to output. occam programs are often designed by making the major processes communicate on a channel, then inserting simple processes like this into the channel to buffer, filter, or transform the transmitted values, almost as if they were electrical components rather than programs.

The logical values **TRUE** and **FALSE** can be used as constants in an occam program, anywhere that a test could be used. So:

```
WHILE TRUE
  INT x :
  SEQ
    input ? x
    output ! x
```

will continue to read values for ever (or until you pull the plug!), whereas:

```
WHILE FALSE
  INT x :
  SEQ
    input ? x
    output ! x
```

is a pointless sort of process which terminates immediately and will read no values at all.

Conditional processes

In addition to repetition, all programming languages need to provide a way for programs to choose to do different things according to a condition i.e. the results of a test. In occam one form of conditional choice is provided by the construction called **IF**.

IF can take any number of processes, each of which has a test placed before it, and make them into a single process. Only one of the component processes will actually be executed, and that will be the first one (in the order in which they are written) whose test is true:

```
IF
  x = 1
    chan1 ! y
  x = 2
    chan2 ! y
```

In this fragment of program (we assume **x**, **y**, **chan1** and **chan2** are declared elsewhere), the value of **y** will either be output on **chan1** or **chan2** depending upon whether the value of **x** is 1 or 2.

The tests **x = 1** and **x = 2** are boolean expressions which are used to choose which component of the **IF** is to be executed. The component parts of the **IF**, each composed of a boolean expression and a process, are called *choices*.

What if the value of **x** were 3? Then the **IF** process would cause the program to stop just as if **STOP** had been executed. The program can only proceed if one of the choices is executed.

(An **IF** with no choices in it just acts like a **STOP**. A **PAR** or **SEQ** with no component processes on the other hand acts like **SKIP** i.e. the program continues as if it were not there at all).

In many cases it will not be acceptable to have the program stop if **x** is not either **1** or **2**. In that case we must add another choice which will be executed no matter what the value of **x**. This is accomplished by using **TRUE**:

```
IF
  x = 1
    chan1 ! y
  x = 2
    chan2 ! y
  TRUE
    chan3 ! y
```

Now **y** will be output on **chan3** if **x** has any other value but **1** or **2**, because the test on the last choice is always true so it will always be executed by default if no previous choice has been executed.

If we wanted nothing to happen at all when **x** was not 1 or 2 we could say:

```
IF
  x = 1
    chan1 ! y
  x = 2
    chan2 ! y
  TRUE
    SKIP
```

This provides one example of the utility of **SKIP**; occam requires some sort of process after the guard and won't allow just blank space.

A better way of writing the above is to explicitly state each case as in the following example:

```
IF
  x = 1
    chan1 ! y
  x = 2
    chan2 ! y
  (x <> 1) AND (x <> 2)
    SKIP
```

Aside: This is a much better way to write conditional processes as it is totally unambiguous. For convenience and simplicity in this tutorial we will, in places, continue to use **TRUE** as a condition. In real programs you should avoid doing so.

To make more complex choices, **IF**s can be nested by using an **IF** process in a choice of another **IF** construct.

```
IF
  x = 1
    chan1 ! y
  x = 2
    IF
      y = 1
        chan2 ! y
      TRUE
        chan3 ! y
  TRUE
    SKIP
```

In this process, **chan3** is used for the output if **x** is **2** and **y** has any other value than **1**.

Selection processes

Like many other programming languages occam provides a further means of making a choice depending upon the value of a variable. Such a construction is called a *selection* in occam and provides an efficient means of selecting one of a number of options in a **CASE**.

CASE can take any number of processes, each of which has a list of one or more expressions placed before it, and combines them into a single process. Only one of the component processes will actually be executed, and that will be the first one (again, in the order in which they are written) with an expression which has the same value as the selecting variable:

```
CASE x
  1
    chan1 ! y
  2
    chan2 ! y
```

In this fragment of program (which is similar to the first example used to describe **IF**), the value of **y** will either be output on **chan1** or **chan2** depending upon whether the value of **x** is 1 or 2. Typically, the constants used in a **CASE** will be named, and also there can be more than one case expression:

```
CASE x
  i, j
    chan1 ! y
  k
    chan2 ! y
```

In this program fragment each constant expression has been given a name: **i**, **j** and **k**. The value of **y** will be output on **chan1** if **x** has the same value as **i** or **j**, and will be output on **chan2** if **x** has the same value as **k**.

What if the value of **x** was none of these values? Then the process would cause the program to stop just as if **STOP** had been executed. The program can only proceed if one of the options is executed, just as an **IF** may only proceed if a choice is executed.

Once again (as we saw with **IF**), in many cases it will not be acceptable to have the program stop if **x** does not have the same value as one of the case expressions. We must then add a further option which will execute no matter what the value of **x**. This is accomplished by using **ELSE**:

```
CASE x
  i, j
    chan1 ! y
  k
    chan2 ! y
  ELSE
    chan3 ! y
```

Now **y** will be output on **chan3** if **x** has any value other than **i**, **j** or **k**.

The component parts of the **CASE**, each composed of an expression and a process, are called *options*.

Alternative processes

In occam, choice has an extra dimension lacking in ordinary programming languages. We have just seen how to make choices according to the values of conditional expressions in a program using **IF**, and how to select an option according to the value of a variable. However we can also make choices according to the state of channels. This is made possible by the **ALT** construction, whose name is short for alternation.

Like **IF**, **ALT** joins together any number of components into a single construction, but the component parts of an **ALT**, called *alternatives* are rather more complicated than **IF** choices.

The simplest kind of **ALT** has as each alternative an input process followed by a process to be executed. The **ALT** watches all the input processes and executes the process associated with the first input to become ready. Thus **ALT** is basically a first-past-the-post race between a group of channels, with only the winner's process being executed:

```
CHAN OF INT chan1, chan2, chan3 :
INT x:
ALT
  chan1 ? x
    ...first process
  chan2 ? x
    ...second process
  chan3 ? x
    ...third process
```

If **chan2** were the first to produce an input, then only the second process would be executed.

Here choice is being decided in the time dimension, the inputs causing the program to wait until one of them is ready.

An alternative may start with a test in addition to an input, just like the tests in an **IF**. If this is done, the associated process can only be chosen if its input is the first to be ready and the test is **TRUE**. occam makes this easy to remember by using the **&** sign, as in:

```
CHAN OF INT chan1, chan2, chan3 :
INT x:
ALT
  (y < 0) & chan1 ? x
    ...first process
  (y = 0) & chan2 ? x
    ...second process
  (y > 0) & chan3 ? x
    ...third process
```

If **y** is, say, **3** and **chan3** is the first to be ready then the third process will be executed. This form of alternative is most often used to impose limits on some process, by using a test such as **(voltage < maximum)**.

As with **IF**, **ALT** behaves like **STOP** if there are no alternatives. Also like **IF**, an **ALT** can be nested as inside an outer **ALT**.

The **ALT** is an extremely powerful construction. It allows complex networks of channels to be merged and switched in a simple and elegant way.

Because of this power, and because it is unlike anything in conventional programming languages, **ALT** is far-and-away the most difficult of the occam constructions to explain and to understand. Fortunately we have now seen enough of occam to be able to work through some more serious examples, which should clarify its usage.

A simple controller program

Let's suppose that we are designing a program to control a portable music centre. Like so many modern appliances it has digital controls rather than rotating knobs.

To control the sound volume, there are two buttons, marked louder and softer. Pressing louder increases the volume one notch, and likewise pressing softer reduces it.

We have two occam channels, also called **louder** and **softer** which produce an input whenever a button is pressed, and a third channel called **amplifier** which transmits a value to the amplifier section, where a control chip sets the volume to that value.

The processes which increase or decrease the volume value are easily written (we'll leave declarations until we have a complete program):

```
SEQ
  volume := volume + 1
  amplifier ! volume
```

and:

```
SEQ
  volume := volume - 1
  amplifier ! volume
```

Now the program needs to decide which button was pressed most recently, and hence which action to take. Combining the two processes in an **ALT** will achieve this:

```
ALT
  louder ? any
    ...increase volume
  softer ? any
    ...decrease volume
```

The actual value sent by the button press is not important, so we'll declare a variable called **any** just to dispose of the input value. As things stand this process will only operate once, on the first button press, and then terminate. It needs to be continually repeated to scan the buttons.

The full program would look like this:

```
INT volume, any :
SEQ
  volume := 0
  amplifier ! volume
  WHILE TRUE
    ALT
      louder ? any
        SEQ
          volume := volume + 1
          amplifier ! volume
      softer ? any
        SEQ
          volume := volume - 1
          amplifier ! volume
```

Notice that **volume** is initially set to 0 so that the volume starts off low, rather than at just any random value.

This program does the job, but using **WHILE TRUE** means that it can never end; when the music centre is switched off the program will just "die" wherever it happens to be at the time. Good programmers don't like that sort of messy ending so let's add another channel which reads the OFF button (call it **off**), and a variable called **active**, which is **TRUE** so long as the music centre is switched on:

```
BOOL active:
INT volume, any :
SEQ
  active := TRUE
  volume := 0
  amplifier ! volume
  WHILE active
    ALT
      louder ? any
        SEQ
          volume := volume + 1
          amplifier ! volume
      softer ? any
        SEQ
          volume := volume - 1
          amplifier ! volume
      off ? any
        active := FALSE
```

This now terminates tidily when the OFF button is pressed.

Aside: For convenience and simplicity in this tutorial we will continue to use **WHILE TRUE** from time to time. In real programs you should avoid doing so, taking good care to ensure correct termination.

As a further refinement we can add tests to the volume increase and decrease processes to limit the values to the range which the control chip can accept (let's say the range is from 0 to 100 units).

We could merely add the tests **volume < 100** and **volume > 0**. As a matter of good programming style though it would be better to define the limits as named constants at the beginning of the program; if the values ever have to be changed (say a new control chip is introduced) then you will only have to change them in one place rather than searching the whole program to find out everywhere they have been used.

The final program looks like this:

```
VAL maximum IS 100 :
VAL minimum IS 0 :
BOOL active :
INT volume, any :
SEQ
  active := TRUE
  volume := minimum
  amplifier ! volume
  WHILE active
    ALT
      (volume < maximum) & louder ? any
        SEQ
          volume := volume + 1
          amplifier ! volume
      (volume > minimum) & softer ? any
        SEQ
          volume := volume - 1
          amplifier ! volume
      off ? any
        active := FALSE
```

The use of named constants can also make a program more readable than if it were strewn with unexplained numbers.

Two points arise from this program:

    1 Notice that we have not declared the channels **louder**, **softer**, **off** and **amplifier**. That's because they connect to the hardware rather than to other occam processes; ultimately they represent physical bits of wire connected to a button. Later on we'll see how to connect channels to hardware in occam.

    2 In a real control program there might be many other things for the program to do besides reading the volume buttons, for example auto-search for selected tunes on a tape. Processes to do these tasks could be combined with the above program using a **PAR** in place of the main **SEQ** so they all proceed at the same time.

Arithmetic in occam

So far we have not discussed what arithmetic operations are available in occam, though we have taken for granted that it has addition, subtraction and multiplication.

The basic arithmetic operations are these:

```
x + y   -- add y to x
x - y   -- subtract y from x
x * y   -- multiply x by y
x / y   -- quotient when x is divided by y
x REM y -- remainder when x is divided by y
```

These operations can be performed on numbers of type **INT** or **REAL**. (see the Formal Definition for precise details of how remainders, overflow and other such matters are treated).

All operators have the same priority in occam so parentheses must be used in complex expressions to enclose component operations and allow them to be treated as single operands. This also establishes the order of evaluation. For example:

```
(2+3)*(4+5)     -- answer 45
 2+(3*(4+5))    -- answer 29
(2+(3*4))+5     -- answer 19
 2+3*4+5        -- illegal
```

The tests are also operators in this sense and so parentheses will be needed to avoid incorrect interpretation. For example:

```
fred = (2+jim)      -- legal expression
(fred+jane) > jim   -- legal expression
fred+jane > jim     -- illegal expression
fred+(jane > jim)   -- illegal expression
                    -- (mixed types)
```

For integers only there is a further set of modulo arithmetic operators. Modulo arithmetic, for those who have not encountered it before, deals with number systems where there is a limited range of numbers. Ordinarily we prefer to think of numbers as going on forever, so that there is always one bigger than any number you can think of.

As an example, (unsigned) arithmetic modulo 8 only allows the numbers 0 to 7 to be used - the result of adding 1 to 7 is zero again. So (5 + 7) modulo 8 is 4. An everyday example of modulo arithmetic is the arithmetic of clock times (modulo 12 or 24 with no zero); adding 3 hours to 11 o'clock gives 2 o'clock, not 14 o'clock.

Modulo arithmetic is important in computers because they always work with numbers that are limited by the size of memory used to store them. For example the largest signed number that can be represented by a 16-bit **INT** is 32,767.

occam has the operators **PLUS**, **MINUS** and **TIMES** for addition, subtraction and multiplication modulo 2^{**}(number of bits in an **INT**).

For boolean truth values, occam has the operators **AND**, **OR** and **NOT** which are defined by:

```
NOT FALSE     = TRUE       NOT TRUE    = FALSE
FALSE AND x = FALSE        TRUE AND x = x
FALSE OR  x = x            TRUE OR  x = TRUE
```

where **x** is any boolean value i.e. either **TRUE** or **FALSE**.

Type conversions

Sometimes it's convenient to convert one type to another in a program; it may for instance save having to declare several extra variables for a value that is only required once. Type conversion should be used sparingly as the whole point of types is to prevent values being used in inappropriate situations.

If **number** has been declared as **INT** and **digit** as **BYTE**, we could still add them together like this:

```
number := ( number * 10 ) + ( INT digit )
```

The reverse conversion, of **INT** to **BYTE** is only legal if the value is within the **BYTE** range of 0 to 255. For example, to output a number between 0 and 9 as a character we could write:

```
output ! BYTE ( number + (INT '0') )
```

Values of type **BOOL** can be converted to type **INT** or **BYTE** and vice versa, using the following definitions:

```
INT TRUE or BYTE TRUE      is 1
INT FALSE or BYTE FALSE    is 0
BOOL 1                     is TRUE
BOOL 0                     is FALSE
```

so if the value of **active** is **FALSE**, **INT active** is 0.

Bit operators

To allow low level operations on the individual bits in a value, occam provides bitwise operators ~ (bitwise not), /\ (bitwise and), \/ (bitwise or) and >< (bitwise exclusive-or) plus the left and right shift operators << and >>. These operators work only on integer values.

Aside: There isn't space here to explain the effect of these operators, which requires knowledge of binary arithmetic. If you are not already familiar with binary arithmetic, any good introductory computing book (e.g. A. Osborne's "An Introduction to Microcomputers - Vol 0") will explain it. But if you don't understand them already, you probably don't need them.

Numeric constants can be entered in hexadecimal notation by preceding them with the **#** sign:

#FE (equivalent to 254 decimal)

This covers occam arithmetic in more than enough depth to follow all the examples in this tutorial. Readers who are greatly concerned with numerical calculations should study the full details presented in the Formal Definition.

Abbreviations

The notation we saw earlier for naming constants (e.g. **VAL maximum IS 1000**) is nothing but a particular form of a more powerful and general device called an abbreviation.

Abbreviations can be used to give a name to any expression in occam, providing a form of universal shorthand. For example:

        VAL exp IS ((x + y) / (fred * 128)) :

defines **exp** to be an abbreviation for the value of the complex expression on the right. The fact that this specification ends with a colon tells us that abbreviations are local, like other occam objects, and their scope is the following process.

An expression abbreviation may, as above, contain variables on its right-hand side, but these variables must remain constant throughout the scope of the abbreviation, and the compiler will report an error if any of the variables are changed (by assignment or input). As a result, an expression abbreviation behaves like a constant throughout its scope.

The full form of an expression abbreviation includes a type before the name:

        VAL INT exp IS ((x + y) / (fred * 128)) :

but this can always be omitted as occam can deduce the type from the types of the values on the right hand side. Programmers may nevertheless wish to sometimes include a type specifier as a reminder of the type of a complicated expression.

occam assumes that numbers below 256 are **INT**s unless told otherwise, which can be done:

        VAL Esc IS 27 (BYTE) :

We shall see later on in Chapter 5 that abbreviations can also be used to name arrays and parts of arrays.

Procedures

A procedure is a process with a name, and this name can be used to represent the procedure in other processes. To define a procedure, the keyword **PROC** and a name is followed by a process which is called the procedure body.

The body of a procedure is executed whenever its name is found in a program; such an occurrence of the name is called an *instance* of the procedure.

A procedure definition looks like this:

```
PROC delay ()              -- procedure heading
  VAL interval IS 1000 :   --
  INT n :                  --
  SEQ                      -- procedure body
    n := interval          --
    WHILE n > 0            --
      n := n - 1           --
:
INT y:                     -- main process
SEQ                        -- starts here
  input1 ? y
  delay ()                 -- instance
  output1 ! y
  delay ()                 -- instance
  input2 ? y
  delay ()                 -- instance
  output2 ! y
```

All this procedure does is to count downwards from 1000 to 0, so it could be used as a crude way of introducing a time delay into a program (the proper way to introduce a delay in occam, using timers, will be introduced later in Chapter 9). The empty parentheses after **delay()** show that this procedure takes no parameters; we'll discuss parameters a little further on.

Note that like all specifications this is attached by a colon to the following process. This tells us that the procedure name obeys the same scope rules as variable and other names - the procedure is only known throughout the process which immediately follows, to which it is linked by the colon. occam puts the colon which ends a procedure definition on a new line, as above, to mark clearly the end of the body. The colon must appear directly below the "P" in **PROC**.

Execution of this program begins at the main process; it reads values from two input channels (assumed to be declared elsewhere), and is delayed for a while before sending them to the output channels. Whenever an instance of delay is encountered, it is executed exactly as if the body of the procedure had been substituted for the name, like this:

```
INT y :
SEQ
  input1 ? y
  VAL interval IS 1000 :
  INT n :
  SEQ
    n := interval
    WHILE n > 0
      n := n - 1
  output1 ! y
  VAL interval IS 1000 :
  INT n :
  SEQ
    n := interval
    WHILE n > 0
      n := n - 1
  input2 ? y
  VAL interval IS 1000 :
  INT n:
  SEQ
    n := interval
    WHILE n > 0
      n := n - 1
  output2 ! y
```

PROC thus provides us with a shorthand; the name **delay** is not only much shorter than the code it replaces, but here it replaces this code three times over. So the main process becomes much more compact, and more readable too since the name **delay** gives us an idea of what it does.

Technical Note: A procedure can always be compiled either by substituting its body as above, or as a closed subroutine.

This is by no means the only benefit bestowed by procedures though. They provide a way of designing better structured programs. By breaking down a program design into the smallest parts which still make sense (called "factorising" the problem), and then writing these parts as procedures, the logic of the whole program is made clearer and easier to follow.

Often such procedures will be used more than once, hence reducing the size of the program, and some may be sufficiently general-purpose to be used again in other programs.

Sensibly factorised programs are easier to modify, debug and maintain because by modifying a single procedure declaration, the changes are automatically effected everywhere in the program that procedure is used.

Hint: There isn't space in this tutorial to cover the subject of structured programming and "top-down" design techniques in proper detail. Readers who are not familiar with these techniques are referred to the numerous books on the subject, of which a recommended example is "Structured Programming" by Dahl, Dijkstra and Hoare.

Parameters

Procedures can be made more useful still by introducing parameters, which allow different values to be passed to different instances of a procedure.

In the delay example above, the length of delay is fixed as **1000** in the text of its definition (by the abbreviation **VAL interval IS 1000**) and it can only be changed by editing the program. A more flexible way would be to pass the delay length as a parameter:

```
      PROC delay (VAL INT interval)
        INT n :
        SEQ
          n := interval
          WHILE n > 0
            n := n - 1
      :
      INT y :                 -- main process
      SEQ                     -- starts here
        input1 ? y
        delay (1000)
        output1 ! y
        delay (2000)
        input2 ? y
        delay (500)
        output2 ! y
```

The name **interval** in the definition of **delay** is called a formal parameter. Formal parameters may be of any type, including **CHAN**, and a type specification is compulsory in the procedure heading. occam cannot read your mind, so it cannot work out what type a formal parameter is meant to be if you don't tell it. (In an abbreviation specification on the other hand, occam has an example value to look at, and so will always be able to deduce its type).

A formal parameter behaves like an abbreviation attached to the procedure body (in fact here it has replaced the abbreviation **VAL interval IS 1000**).

When the procedure body is substituted for an instance of the procedure name in a process, this formal parameter name becomes an abbreviation for a value called the actual parameter. In the above example, the actual parameters are **1000**, **2000** and **500**. In the first case **interval** becomes an abbreviation for **1000** throughout the procedure body so **delay (1000)** has exactly the same effect as our original non-parameterised procedure.

A procedure can have any number of formal parameters, which must be separated by commas in the definition heading. The actual parameters of an instance are similarly separated by commas. One actual parameter must be supplied for each formal parameter, and they correspond by position (the first actual parameter matches the first formal etc.):

```
PROC box.volume (VAL INT length, breadth, depth)
  ... body                      -- definition
:
box.volume (24, 16, 20)         -- instance
```

Procedures with parameters provide a still more powerful shorthand, for now we can use the same procedure in different places with different internal values. In the above program for instance, the second delay will last twice as long as the first and the third will last half as long.

We are not limited to calling **delay** with constants like **1000** as the actual parameter. Any variable of type **INT** could be used as an actual parameter e.g. **delay (x)**.

Occam parameter passing convention

In occam, when a variable is passed as an actual parameter to a procedure, it is as if the variable replaces the formal parameter throughout the procedure. Anything that is done to the formal parameter, is done to the variable, which may therefore have its value changed.

Take this example:

```
PROC decrement (INT number)
  number := number - 1
:
```

If we use **decrement (x)** as an instance of the procedure, the value of **x** will be reduced by one when **decrement (x)** terminates.

Take care: This behaviour differs from that found in certain other widely used languages. The commonly used call-by-value convention (available in C and Pascal) has the effect of evaluating the variable (actual) parameter, and using the result as the initial value of the formal parameter, which behaves as a local variable of the procedure body. Consequently, an assignment to the formal parameter has no effect on the actual parameter. The occam convention is more nearly equivalent to Pascal's call-by-reference (or VAR) parameters. This point is emphasised because it may trip up programmers who are experienced in these other languages.

Sometimes it is preferable that a procedure should not alter the value of a variable passed to it as a parameter. We have already seen how to achieve this in our delay example; decant the value of the parameter into a local variable (**n** in the example) and do any manipulations on this local value. Use this method if you need to translate Pascal procedures or similar with value parameters, into occam.

If only the original value of a variable is needed in a procedure, i.e. if the formal parameter is never altered by assignment or input, then a more efficient program may result if we explicitly say that only the value is to be passed, using **VAL**:

```
PROC delay (VAL INT limit)
  INT n :
  SEQ
    n := 0
    WHILE n < limit
      n := n + 1
:
```

When **VAL** is used like this, the formal parameter can be thought of as representing a constant throughout the procedure body, and the compiler (after checking that it's true) may exploit the fact to produce more efficient code.

The volume controller program we developed in the last section could be rewritten using a procedure:

```
VAL step.up IS 1 :
VAL step.down IS -1 :
BOOL active :
INT volume, any :
PROC change.volume (VAL INT step)
  SEQ
    volume := volume + step
    amplifier ! volume
:
SEQ
  volume := 0
  amplifier ! volume
  active := TRUE
  WHILE active
    ALT
      louder ? any
        change.volume (step.up)
      softer ? any
        change.volume (step.down)
      off ? any
        active := FALSE
```

Notice that a single procedure now serves both to increase and decrease the volume.

Another point to note is that this **PROC** body uses the variable **volume** even though that variable is not declared in the **PROC**, either as a local variable or a formal parameter. This is quite acceptable to occam; **volume** is called a *free* variable with respect to **PROC change.volume** and has the useful property of being able to retain its value from one call of the procedure to the next, which is precisely why it is used here. Note that **volume** must be declared somewhere before the **PROC** definition, otherwise occam would reject it as an undeclared name.

A variable is free with respect to a procedure when the procedure is defined inside the scope of the variable.

Functions

Most conventional languages support functions. Briefly, a function is a process which returns a value and thus may be used in expressions. Many functions are mathematical, and return such things as the sine and cosine of their arguement. There is a big difference between the type of functions mathematicans know and love, and functions as known by most programmers (which are nowhere near as trustworthy). occam provides the more trustworthy kind of function.

In occam a function gives a name to a special kind of process which returns a result, called a *value process*. occam functions have the advantage of being side effect free. Practically, this means that occam is very strict about how you construct functions. The great advantage of this however, is that when you use a function you can guarantee it will have no effect upon any other part of your program. Many of the bugs which mysteriously appear in programs written in other languages are due to the fact that you cannot make the same guarantees.

Function definitions take the general form:

> *type* **FUNCTION** *name* ({ , *formal parameter* })
>   *specification* :
> **VALOF**
>   *process*
>   **RESULT** *expression*

And, for example, a function which returns the value of the largest of two integers would look like this:

```
INT FUNCTION max (VAL INT a, b)
  INT answer:
  VALOF
    IF
      a > b
        answer := a
      b > a
        answer := b
      a = b
        answer := a   -- could in fact be either value
    RESULT answer
  :
```

Notice that a type specifier precedes the keyword **FUNCTION**. This is important as it specifies the type of the value returned by the function.

The formal parameters of a function can only be value (**VAL**) parameters. **PAR**allel and **ALT**ernation constructs cannot be used within the function. Also input and output must not be used within the function. You can only assign to variables declared within the scope of the function; "free variables" can be read but not assigned to. Only procedures defined within the scope of the function and adhering to the above rules may be used.

A function returns a value and is defined as an operand, so functions can appear where-ever an expression would appear. Using our function to return the maximum of two values in an assignment for example:

```
x := max (a, b)
```

Or in an expression to gain twice the maximum value:

```
x := max (a, b) * 2
```

Functions share many of the advantages of procedures and extend the facility to factorise programs written in occam.

Hint: There isn't space in this tutorial to go into functions in any great depth or to cover the many issues involved. A full description of functions in occam can be found in the occam *2 Reference manual* published by INMOS.

5 Arrays in occam

An array is a group of objects of the same type, joined into a single object with a name. Each object in an array can be individually referred to by stating the number of its position in the array - such a number is called an array subscript, and the individual object it refers to is called a component of the array.

In occam array variables are declared in the same way as single variables of any type, but with the number of components in brackets prefixed to the type specifier:

```
[20]INT fred:        -- an array of twenty integers called fred
[100]CHAN OF INT switchboard: -- an array of 100 channels
                              -- called switchboard
[12]BOOL jury:       -- an array of 12 truth values called jury
```

Technical Note: In occam the size of an array must be fixed when the program is compiled; it cannot be decided or changed while the program is running.

A component of such an array variable is selected by stating the array name suffixed with the subscript number in brackets. Subscripts start at zero, so the first component in an array is component 0. Here are some sample array components:

```
fred[0]            -- the first integer in fred
switchboard[20]    -- the 21st channel in switchboard
jury[11]           -- the last component of jury
```

Take care: Attempting to use a subscript which is larger than the size of an array (e.g. `fred[200]`) will cause an error, but exactly how and when this error is reported may vary between different implementations of occam.

Components of array variables behave just like ordinary variables of the same type and can be used anywhere a variable could be used. They can be assigned or input to, and output to a channel:

```
chan1 ? fred[15]     -- input from chan1 to
                     --    the 16th component of fred
jury[4] := TRUE      -- assign TRUE to the 5th component of jury
switchboard[99] ! fred[1] -- output the 2nd component of fred
                          -- on the last switchboard channel
```

By way of example, here is a process to read values from a channel (declared in another process) into the successive components of an array:

```
INT index :
[100]INT array :
SEQ
  index := 0
  WHILE index < 100
    SEQ
      chan1 ? array[index]
      index := index + 1
```

Whole array variables may also be input, output or assigned to in occam, with the proviso that for input and assignment, the receiving variable must be an array of the same type, and the protocol of the channel used must be compatible with the type of the array.

Array types

The type of an array reflects both its size and the type of its components, so the type of **fred** is [20] INT.

The whole array **fred** could be sent to another process like this:

```
PAR
  comm ! fred
  ...more processes
  comm ? jane
```

if **jane** is an array of type [20] INT. The channel **comm** would need to be declared as:

```
CHAN OF [20] INT comm :
```

that is, the type of data values passed on the channel must be type [20] INT.

Arrays may be used as parameters to procedures. occam, in contrast to many languages, does not require the size of an array parameter to be specified when the procedure is declared, which means that an array of any size, but of the correct data type, may be passed as an actual parameter.

This is an extremely powerful property, which allows the same procedure to manipulate arrays of any size. The type specifier for an array formal parameter looks like an array type with the size omitted (e.g. [] INT, which means an array of INTs of any size).

Since a procedure needs to know how big an array it has been given, occam provides the operator SIZE, which measures the size of an array:

```
PROC read.in (CHAN OF INT input, []INT array)
  INT index :
  SEQ
    index := 0
    WHILE index < (SIZE array)
      SEQ
        input ? array[index]
        index := index + 1
:
```

This procedure, which reads in single values from a channel to an array, can be legally called with an integer array of any size, say **read.in (switchboard[12], fred)**. SIZE always produces a value of type INT.

Array segments

A segment of an array is expressed using the form:

[*array* FROM *subscript* FOR *count*]

Both *subscript* and *count* may be variables.

A segment of an array consists of several consecutively numbered components of the array. As a result, the segment can itself be treated as an array. As an example **[fred FROM 10 FOR 5]** would be an array composed of the five components **fred[10]** to **fred[14]**. **[fred FROM 0 FOR 20]** would select the whole array and is the same as writing **fred**.

Array segments may be input, output or assigned to, but as with whole arrays, only if the expression which is assigned is an array of the same type as the segment. This is legal:

```
[fred FROM 10 FOR 5] := [fred FROM 1 FOR 5]
```

and so would be:

```
[fred FROM 10 FOR 5]  := jane
```

if **jane** had been declared as [5]INT.

Tables

occam provides a powerful means of generating an array value, called a table. If **x** is a variable of type INT, and its current value is 10, the table:

```
[x,  x+1,  x+2,  x+3]
```

generates an array of type [4]INT and value [10, 11, 12, 13].

This array can be assigned to a variable:

```
INT x :
[4]INT xarray :
SEQ
   ...
   xarray := [x, x+1, x+2, x+3]
```

or subscripted directly:

```
chan3 ! [x, x+1, x+2, x+3][2]
```

or abbreviated to a name for later use:

```
INT x :
...
VAL xarray IS [x, x+1, x+2, x+3] :
SEQ
   ...
   chan3 ! xarray[2]
```

More on abbreviations

Since the description of an array segment or table becomes rather cumbersome if it has to be referred to often in a program, the use of abbreviations is to be encouraged.

The declaration:

```
f IS [fred FROM 10 FOR 5]  :
```

allows **f** to be treated as an array of size **5** with subscripts running from 0 to **4**. So **f[2]** refers to the same component as **fred[12]**.

Notice that **VAL** is not used, as it is when abbreviating a constant or expression; we are not merely naming a value here. An abbreviation for an array, array component, array segment or simple variable behaves just like the object itself. In other words it is permissible to change the value of the object referred to by the abbreviation name, either by assignment or input.

The array assignment example above could thus be written more succinctly as:

```
f := jane
```

What is not permissible, in the case of an abbreviation for an array component or array segment, is to alter which component or components are referred to. So if we declare an abbreviation like:

```
line IS switchboard[i] :
```

then it is illegal to change the value of the subscript i within the scope of line. line must always refer to the same component of switchboard, defined by the value of i at the time it was specified. Similar considerations would apply if lines were a segment of switchboard defined by two variable subscripts.

In short, an abbreviation for a component of a subscripted array behaves like the component itself, with a constant subscript, throughout the scope of the abbreviation.

Technical Note: Such use of abbreviations can often bring performance benefits as well as conciseness. Using an abbreviation for an array component inside an inner loop, instead of subscripting the array, has two beneficial consequences.

1 The compiler recognises that the subscripts are constant and so does not compile runtime range checks.

2 The address of the array component becomes local to the loop process, rather than global, and occam processes handle local data faster than global.

An abbreviation can also be used to set up an array constant such as:

```
VAL powers2 IS [1,2,4,8,16,32,64,128] :
```

The components of powers2 can be accessed just as in any other array so powers2[3] is 8.

VAL must be used when defining an array constant or table abbreviation, to indicate that only the values of the components, rather than the components themselves are being referred to. The effect is that these components become read-only; they may not have their values changed.

Multidimensional arrays

occam supports arrays with any number of dimensions and they are declared in a way consistent with what we have seen so far. A two dimensional array resembles a table, in which any component can be referred to by supplying two subscripts, to specify which row and column it occupies. If only one subscript is supplied then a whole row is accessed at once i.e. the value is a single dimensioned array.

For instance a chess board can be simulated by a two dimensional array of 8 rows by 8 columns i.e. 64 components. It could be declared in occam as:

```
[8][8]BYTE chessboard:
```

If we create constants to represent the pieces:

```
VAL empty        IS 0 (BYTE) :
VAL black.pawn   IS 1 (BYTE) :
VAL black.knight IS 2 (BYTE) :
VAL black.rook   IS 3 (BYTE) :
...
```

then a program could set up the board like this:

```
chessboard[0][2] := white.bishop
```

and a move would look like:

```
chessboard[3][4] := chessboard[4][5]
chessboard[4][5] := empty
```

Tables can be used to generate multi-dimensional array values. For example, a two-dimensional array constant could be given the name **curve** by this abbreviation:

```
VAL curve IS [[0,0],[1,1],[2,4],[3,9],[4,16]] :
```

The value of **curve[2]** is **[2,4]** and the value of **curve[2][1]** is 4.

6 Channel communication

occam programming is mainly concerned with communication between processes, and channels are the primary means by which this communication takes place. It is therefore important that channels should be able to carry data of any type. We have seen in Chapter 2 that channels must be specified to be of a certain type, just as variables are.

It is equally important however that channels should be able to carry data of mixed types when required; otherwise we would find that we had to declare several channels of different types just to achieve a single communication, and large unwieldy programs would result. One solution would be to make channels unchecked, but this would hinder the compiler in its efforts to create efficient and secure programs.

occam instead provides a number of ways for grouping types together and creating a *protocol* for communication. Such a protocol can be used to specify the sequence of types of object that may be sent down a channel. In effect a protocol is a template which describes the format of messages composed of groups of occam data types. The protocol for a channel is specified by type of channel declared:

```
CHAN OF protocol name:
```

Every input and output on a channel must be compatible with the protocol of the channel, which means it must match it in both the type and the number of objects. Incompatible inputs and outputs will be detected by the compiler and signalled as errors.

Simple protocol

The simplest kind of protocol consists merely of a primitive type, such as we have been using so far. The declaration:

```
CHAN OF INT comm :
```

means that channel **comm** may only carry single values of integer type, while:

```
CHAN OF [20]INT x :
```

permits **x** only to carry arrays of **20** integers.

Inputs and outputs from channels with simple protocols are only legal if the receiving or sending variable is of the type specified by the protocol. The program fragment:

```
[30]INT x :
CHAN OF [20]INT y :
SEQ
  y ? x
```

results in an error because **x** is not of the type specified by the protocol of **y**.

Naming protocols

Protocol requirements can become more complex, and require the communication of a sequence of simple protocols. Such a sequential protocol is given a name in a protocol definition.

```
PROTOCOL Word IS INT :
PROTOCOL Pair IS INT ; INT :
. . . .
CHAN OF Word words:
CHAN OF Pair pairs:
```

Sequential protocol

A sequential protocol specifies that a certain sequence of values, possibly of mixed types, may be sent over a channel.

For example, the protocol definition and declaration:

```
PROTOCOL Message IS BYTE; INT; INT:
...
CHAN OF Message comm :
```

says that **comm** may only carry messages consisting of a byte value followed by two integers. So **40 (BYTE) ; 999; 505** could legally be output on **comm** but **999; 505; 40 (BYTE)** could not (starts with an **INT**) and neither could **40 (BYTE) ; 999; 505; 234** (too many values).

In general, a sequential protocol is just a list of any number of types, all separated by semicolons.

A value to be output on channels with a specified sequential protocol, can be constructed by listing the component values separated by semicolons:

```
comm ! 40(BYTE); 999; 505
```

In a similar way a sequential protocol can be input as:

```
comm ? x; y; z
```

A program which sends records of numbers over a channel might look like:

```
PROTOCOL Message IS BYTE; INT; INT:
CHAN OF Message comm :
PAR
  SEQ
    ... processes
    comm ! 40(BYTE); 999; 505
  BYTE x :
  INT y, z :
  SEQ
    comm ? x; y; z
    ... more processes
```

Variable length array protocol

One particular kind of protocol is so commonly used that a special type has been provided for it. In the above section on Primitive types it was stressed that arrays may only be sent over a channel with a protocol of the same type. This is a very restrictive requirement, especially as we have seen that occam permits arrays of arbitrary size to be passed as parameters to procedures.

Accordingly a special kind of simple protocol is provided, which concisely permits the size of an array to be sent before the array itself. Such a protocol is defined as:

type1 :: *type2*

which says that the channel can carry pairs of values consisting of a size value of *type1* followed by that number of components, corresponding to the first components in the specified array type. A channel capable of carrying integer arrays of any size could be declared as:

```
CHAN OF INT::[]INT comm :
```

or, if only arrays of up to 255 elements are anticipated, as:

```
CHAN OF BYTE::[]INT comm :
```

The following process outputs two integer arrays of differing sizes on the same channel:

```
CHAN OF INT::[]INT comm :
[20]INT fred :
[35]INT jane :
SEQ
   comm ! 20::fred
   comm ! 35::jane
```

A corresponding input process is as follows:

```
INT size :
[256]INT array :
SEQ
   comm ? size::array
   ...
   comm ? size::array
```

The above process is invalid if an attempt is made to input an array larger than the size of **array**.

occam treats variable length array protocols just like other simple protocols. They may therefore be used as components in sequential protocols. For example the protocol in this declaration:

```
PROTOCOL Doubles IS BYTE::[]BYTE; BYTE::[]BYTE :
```

allows a channel to carry pairs of arrays of bytes. Such arrays, as we shall see in the next chapter, can be used to represent text strings so this channel could carry pairs of English words.

Variant protocol

Sequential protocols permit us to specify the format of the messages which can be sent between two occam processes over a channel. Often however it will be convenient for a single channel to be able to carry messages of several different formats. This is possible if we use a variant protocol.

A variant protocol is, in effect, a set of different protocols, any one of which may be used when communicating on the channel. Each of these protocols must be identified in some way, and this is done by giving them tags. A tagged protocol is simply a protocol whose first component is a unique name which identifies the protocol. The set of tagged protocols is grouped together in a **CASE** construct. Variant protocols are always given a name by a protocol definition. The following definition defines a variant protocol with the name **Messages**:

```
PROTOCOL Messages
   CASE
      a; INT
      b; BYTE; INT
      c; BYTE; BYTE
:
```

where **a**, **b** and **c** are the respective tags. A declaration of a channel with this variant protocol set looks like this:

```
CHAN OF Messages comm :
```

The meaning is quite straightforward; **comm** may carry messages of variant **a**, or of variant **b**, or of variant **c**.

When inputting from a channel which has a variant type, it is necessary to know which of the possible kinds of message has actually been sent. The purpose of the tag is to enable us to perform this identification.

It is not possible to simply perform an input from the channel because we cannot decide what type (or number) of receiving variables to use. For instance:

```
INT x :
SEQ
  comm ? x
```

would be compatible with a message of variant **a** above, but not with a message of variant **b** or **c**.

Case input

To perform such an input, occam provides a case input. Take for example:

```
PROTOCOL Message
  CASE
    a; INT; INT
    b; BYTE::[]BYTE
:
CHAN OF Message comm :
PAR
  INT x, y :
  BYTE size :
  [256]BYTE v :
  comm ? CASE
    a; x; y        -- input to variant a
      ... process
    b; size::v     -- input to variant b
      ... process
```

The other processes in the **PAR** may now send messages such as:

```
comm ! a; 100; 250
```

or:

```
comm ! b; 5::"hello"
```

and the above input selection will correctly receive either kind of message, by first inspecting its tag and then performing the appropriate input process with receiving variables of the correct type.

A case input can be used as a guard process in an **ALT** construction.

```
INT x, y :
BYTE size :
[256]BYTE v :
ALT
  comm ? CASE
    a; x; y        -- input to variant a
      ... process
    b; size::v     -- input to variant b
      ... process
  ... more alternatives
```

Known input

In processes where the input is a single known component of a variant protocol the following kind of fixed input may be used

```
comm ? CASE a; x; y
```

This will cause an error if an input of any structure other than that defined by the tag **a** is attempted.

Tag-only types

It is sometimes useful to declare channels which accept nothing but tags. For instance the channel:

```
PROTOCOL Tags
  CASE
    one
    two
    three
:
CHAN OF Tags signal :
```

can only carry one of the three tags **one**, **two** or **three**.

```
signal ? CASE
  one
    ... action 1
  two
    ... action 2
  three
    ... action 3
```

In the chapter on **ALT** we saw the use of a variable called **any** to receive and dispose of an arbitrary input value from a channel which functioned purely as a signal. A more concise and rigorous way of creating such a signal channel is to limit its protocol, and hence the traffic it can carry, to a single signal value:

```
PROTOCOL Command
  CASE
    play
    dance
    quit
:
CHAN OF Command signal :
BOOL going :
...
SEQ
  going := TRUE
  WHILE going
    signal ? CASE
      play
        ... hamlet
      dance
        ... tango
      quit
        going := FALSE
```

The **quit** signal would be issued by another process using the output:

```
signal ! quit
```

This is inherently more secure than the **any** method. The compiler can detect any erroneous attempt to send a value other than **play**, **dance** or **quit** down the **signal** channel because it would violate the channel's protocol.

7 Characters and strings

Character strings are used in computer languages to represent text data such as words and sentences. "The cat sat on the mat" is a single string of 22 characters to most computer languages, the spaces being characters just as the letters are.

Aside: Characters are represented in a computer as numbers, using a coding system which allocates a unique number to each letter of the alphabet (both upper and lower case), the numerals, the punctuation marks (including space) and various special characters like $, % and @. The most common coding for small computers is ASCII (American Standard Code for Information Interchange). occam uses the ASCII standard code with a guaranteed subset.

It would be tedious in the extreme if text could only be handled by translating each letter into a number, so occam allows two notations for describing text data.

Single characters may be written as the character contained in single quotes e.g. `'a'`. Such a constant is translated into a one byte number by occam.

A text string may be written in double quotes e.g. `"antidisestablishmentarianism"`. occam translates such a string constant into a table of type `[n]BYTE` where **n** is the length of the string. The value of the string `"hello"` is equivalent to the value of the table `['h', 'e', 'l', 'l', 'o']`.

When text is output on a printer or VDU screen certain codes like carriage return, newline and tab don't produce a printed symbol but instead affect the way the following text is printed. For example the newline character causes subsequent output to continue on the line below the current position.

Because these codes don't have a printing symbol, occam gives them a special representation so that you can include them in strings. For instance newline is represented as `*n` and tab is `*t`. More generally any character can be represented by an asterisk followed by its code in hexadecimal notation. For more details see the Formal Definition at the rear of this book.

String constants can be assigned to arrays, and manipulated in a variety of ways. Single characters can be selected from them by ordinary subscripting, or whole parts of the string may be selected as an array segment.

As an illustration, here is a function which returns a pointer to the first occurrence of a given character found in a string:

```
INT FUNCTION find.char (VAL BYTE char,
                        VAL []BYTE string)
  INT index :
  VALOF
    SEQ
      index := 0
      WHILE (index < (SIZE string)) AND
            (char <> string[index])
        index := index + 1
    RESULT index
:
```

An occurrence of our function in the assignment:

```
c := find.char ('a',"dingaling")
```

causes **c** to become **4**, which is the subscript of the letter **a** in the string `"dingaling"`. Note that if the character is not found the function returns a value equal to the length of the string. A more elegant way to express this function is given later in the chapter on *replicators*.

String output

Since strings are merely arrays, they can be sent over channels in one chunk, provided that the variable used for input is an array of the right length and the channel has a suitable protocol.

If we declare an array **string** to be large enough to hold any **string** we need to send, then it can be "tailored" to individual strings by sending the size first:

```
PROTOCOL String IS BYTE::[]BYTE :
CHAN OF  String comm :
PAR
  SEQ
    ...
    VAL message IS "England expects" :
    comm ! BYTE(SIZE message)::message
    ...
  [80]BYTE string :
  BYTE size :
  SEQ
    comm ? size::string
    ...
```

Note that here we have chosen to restrict the count to byte size (hence the type conversion **BYTE (SIZE message)**) and only strings of 255 or less characters can be sent.

Strings can also be output a character at a time, by using a subscript in a loop:

```
PROC output.string (CHAN OF BYTE out, []BYTE message)
  INT i :
  SEQ
    i := 0
    WHILE i < (SIZE message)
      SEQ
        out ! message[i]
        i := i + 1
:
```

Though this appears to be less efficient than the previous block output method, it has the advantage that the characters of the string become individually available, and so could be processed in some way. A variation of this procedure could, for example, convert the string to upper-case before output.

Lower-case ASCII characters have codes which are larger by 32 than the upper-case character code (e.g. **'a'** is ASCII code 97, while **'A'** is 65). Expressed in binary, this means that the sixth bit is 1 in the lower-case version, but is 0 in the upper-case. To make any character upper-case (leaving it unchanged if already upper) therefore we need to /\ (bitwise and) it with binary 11011111, i.e.

hexadecimal **DF**, to set this bit to 0:

```
PROC output.ucstring (CHAN OF BYTE out, []BYTE message)
  INT i :
  SEQ
    i := 0
    WHILE i < (SIZE message)
      SEQ
        out ! message[i] /\ #DF
        i := i + 1
:
```

In both of these latter two procedures we are sending the string as a stream of **BYTE**s (so any actual channel parameter must be of type **CHAN OF BYTE**) and no size information is sent. This raises the question of how any receiving process would know that the stream had ended. If it tried to keep inputting characters once the **WHILE** in the output procedure had terminated, deadlock would result.

One solution is to send the size of the string as the first item, as in previous examples. Another would be to send a special "end-of-stream" character after the **WHILE** finishes. For example:

```
PROC input.string (CHAN OF BYTE in, []BYTE message)
  INT i :
  SEQ
    i := 0
    WHILE message[i] <> end.of.file.char
      SEQ
        in ? message[i]
        i := i + 1
:
```

Our output routine would need to complete its output with a suitable, "end of file character".

```
out ! end.of.file.char
```

8 Replicators

One of the most powerful features of occam is that it allows the construction of arrays of processes in addition to data and channel arrays.

A novel device called the replicator is used together with one of the occam constructs **SEQ**, **PAR**, **ALT** and **IF** to create an array of similar processes of the corresponding kind. Individual processes in a replicated construct can be referred to using the replicator index, in just the same way that components of an array are selected using a subscript. The general form of a replicator is:

REP index = base **FOR** *count*
    process

where *REP* is one of **SEQ**, **PAR**, **ALT** or **IF**. **Take care**: If the *count* in a replicator is zero, the process behaves like a single construct with no components i.e. **SEQ** will act like **SKIP** (do nothing) but **IF** and **ALT** act like **STOP** (stop the process).

Replicated SEQ

Lets start with the most straightforward replicated construct, the replicated **SEQ**. If **input** is specified as a channel then:

```
INT x:
SEQ i = 0 FOR 5
  input ? x
```

says "create five replicas of the input process and execute them in sequence". The effect is as if we had written:

```
INT x:
SEQ
   input ? x
   input ? x
   input ? x
   input ? x
   input ? x
```

which in its turn is as if we had specified a loop with five iterations:

```
INT x, i:
SEQ
  i := 0
  WHILE i < 5
    SEQ
      input ? x
      i := i + 1
```

In other words, a replicated **SEQ** is equivalent to a counted loop. Using a replicated **SEQ** is more concise than using **WHILE** because there's no need to specify and increment an index variable and test its value each time round.

The replicator index variable, which can be given any name, increases by one from the base value for count times, and can be used to reference a particular pass through the loop. Note that the index does not need to be separately specified, and is always of type **INT**. An array of any size could be filled with input values like this:

```
SEQ i = 0 FOR SIZE big.array
  input ? big.array[i]
```

which has the same effect as:

```
SEQ
   input ? big.array[0]
   input ? big.array[1]
   ...........
   input ? big.array[(SIZE big.array) - 1]
```

occam allows either or both base and count values in a replicated **SEQ** to be variables rather than constants.

Take care: It is forbidden to input or assign to the replicator index. There is no way to cause partial execution of a replicated **SEQ** (or any other replicated construct); remember that they are not loops but arrays of processes which only terminate when all their processes have terminated.

Replicated PAR

A replicated **PAR** builds an array of structurally similar parallel processes. Any process can be referred to by means of the replicator index.

The replicated **PAR** is of paramount importance in occam programming. Used in conjunction with an array of channels, it permits economical and elegant expression of some of the stock data structures used by programmers, such as buffers and queues, but furthermore it allows the exploitation of multiple concurrent processors using pipelining and other techniques.

Technical Note: Current implementations of occam do not allow the count in a replicated **PAR** to be a variable value. This is in order that the compiler can know all the resources needed by a process at compile time.

As an example let's look first at a simple queue. A queue is precisely what you would expect from the everyday meaning of the word, a structure through which a number of values pass, with the first value to arrive being also the first value to leave:

```
——————▶ $     $$$$$$$$$$$$$$$$$$$$     ——————▶ $
incoming          queue of length 20      outgoing
  value                                      value
```

Queues are used extensively in programming, often as buffers for processes which consume data more slowly than they are being supplied. In order that no data should be lost, they are buffered or queued to wait their turn. Such buffers are often called FIFO buffers, short for First In/ First Out.

A typical application would be in a computer terminal's keyboard. Some programs may accept characters slower than a fast typist can enter them. If a queue is used to accept the characters, then users can type as fast as they wish, the queue growing as they type ahead of the program.

In occam a queue can be simulated by an array of parallel processes passing data from one to the other like a bucket chain:

```
[21]CHAN OF INT slot :
PAR i = 0 FOR 20
   WHILE TRUE
     INT x :
     SEQ
       slot[i] ? x
       slot[i+1] ! x
```

The replicated **PAR** sets up 20 parallel processes each of which continually transfers values between two slots in the queue, which is represented by an array of 21 channels. The net effect is that each value has to pass through the whole queue before leaving from `slot[20]`:

As it stands this is not a complete program, because the first process in the queue needs somewhere to input its values from, and the last process needs somewhere to output to. Otherwise each will be waiting, and the whole queue will be deadlocked. We assume that the queue is part of a larger program which feeds data into `slot[0]` and bleeds data from `slot[20]`, like this:

```
PAR
  ...feed
  ...queue
  ...bleed
```

If the supply of data were temporarily interrupted, data already in the queue would continue to be passed along, the earlier processes waiting automatically by the very nature of the occam input process.

When the supply starts again, the early processes can proceed, but later processes will now be waiting. Thus it is possible for processes anywhere in the line to be waiting even as the flow of data goes on - only if the queue is allowed to become empty or full will all the processes be waiting.

A type-ahead buffer program could look something like:

```
[41]CHAN OF INT typeahead.buff :
PROC keyboard.input ( )
  WHILE TRUE
    INT x :
    SEQ
      keyboard ? x
      typeahead.buff[0] ! x
:
PROC queue ( )
  PAR i = 0 FOR 40
    WHILE TRUE
      INT x :
      SEQ
        typeahead.buff[i] ? x
        typeahead.buff[i+1] ! x
:
PROC terminal.output ( )
  WHILE TRUE
    INT x :
    SEQ
      typeahead.buff[40] ? x
      terminal ! x
:
PAR                         -- main program
  keyboard.input ( )
  queue ( )
  terminal.output ( )
```

Here it's assumed that **keyboard** and **terminal** are channels which already exist in the system; we shall see more on this topic in Chapter 9.

Hint: Please study these examples carefully, if necessary working through them with pencil and paper until you thoroughly understand them. Replicated **PAR** exemplifies the occam approach to programming and its difference from conventional languages.

Pipelined processing

The pipeline goes a step beyond the simple queue; it more resembles a factory production line than a bucket chain. Instead of merely passing data from one slot to another unchanged, a pipeline transforms the data it passes.

Problems suitable for processing by a replicated **PAR** pipeline are those which can be broken down into a number of simple identical steps. A pipeline then consists of this number of "processors" arranged in a linear array, each capable of performing one step.

Raw data is fed into the pipeline, and a finished result is produced from the far end. In between, the transformation is performed one step at a time on the passing data.

How is this better than a simple loop which performs the required number of steps? Because much of the processing of successive steps can proceed at the same time. The individual steps are overlapped in time, and new data can be fed into the pipeline as soon as the first step is complete rather than waiting until all the steps have been completed.

The analogy with a car production line is instructive. At each workstation on such a line, some component gets bolted onto a car (represented in the following diagram by the letters **A..E**). When the line is running properly there will be a car at each workstation in a different stage of construction:

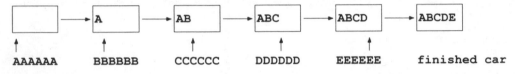

The throughput of cars would obviously be much slower if only one car passed down the line at once, a new one not being put on until the first was finished. But this is precisely what happens in a simple program loop.

The speed advantage produced by pipelining is due to this overlapping of processes. A single value takes just as long to pass through the line as it would if processed by a simple loop. The saving of time is thus zero for a single value, and only shows up when there is a stream of numbers to process; successive numbers will be available at much shorter intervals from a pipeline. In diagrammatic form:

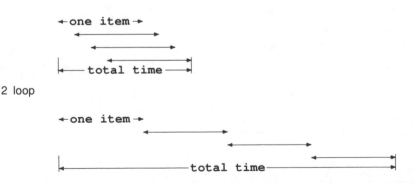

Aside: The time savings can be dramatic; in principle the time to process *n* numbers using a pipeline can be better than *n* times faster than a single processor, because by using smaller local memories, the memory fetch time can be reduced (cf. the car workers have less far to fetch the components). But don't forget that the maximum time saving is only obtained when each stage of the pipeline has its own processor. Simulated pipelining on a single processor by time sharing achieves little, as the speed of each stage is reduced in proportion; you can't have something for nothing. Pipelined processing is used in supercomputers such as the Cray 1 to perform fast multiple precision arithmetic, using hardware array processors.

occam allows this form of pipelining to be described using the replicated **PAR**. The resulting program could be run on a single processor, or using a separate processor for each stage, or any combination in between these extremes. To illustrate the method we shall develop a pipeline program to sort values into order.

A pipelined sort program

The basic principle of the program will be that a stream of unsorted numbers is passed into a pipeline which has as many parallel processes as there are numbers. Each replicated process has local variables called **highest** and **next**.

As a number enters a new process, it will be compared with the value in **highest**. If it is not larger than **highest**, then it will be passed straight on to the next process in the pipe. If it is larger than **highest** then it will be kept i.e. it will be put into **highest** and the previous value of **highest** will be sent on to the next process in its stead. When all the numbers have been through the process, the final value of **highest** is passed on.

By this means the numbers gradually "sediment out" with the "heaviest", i.e. largest, being held back in the stream. In the first process the largest number migrates to the last position in the stream, in the second process the second largest migrates to the second from last, and so on adding one sorted number to the back of stream at each stage.

Work through an example with pencil and paper to convince yourself that it works, something along these lines:

```
                                  1st process
   unsorted        highest    next
   5 2 8 4 7   →       7        4  ───────────→ 4
                       7        8  ──────────→ 7
                       8        2  ─────────→ 2
                       8        5  ───────→ 5
                       8          →  8

                                  2nd process
   8 5 2 7 4   →       4        7  ───────────→ 4
                       7        2  ─────────→ 2
                       7        5  ───────→ 5
                       7        8  ─────→ 7
                       8          →  8
   8 7 5 2 4   →     etc.
```

Overall the pipeline looks like this:

```
   5 2 8 4 7        ──→ P0 ──→ P1 ──→ P2 ──→ P3 ──→ P4 ──→      8 7 5 4 2
                     c0      c1      c2      c3      c4      c5
```

where **P** means process and **c** means channel.

We'll write an example program to sort 100 numbers. First of all we need to define an array of channels to form the pipeline:

```
[101]CHAN OF INT pipe :
```

Note that as in the queue example above, we need one more channel than the number of processes; the last diagram makes clear why.

At the heart of the program is the process which compares values. For the i'th pipe of the pipeline, it can be written:

```
SEQ
  pipe[i] ? next           -- input next value
  IF
    next <= highest        -- not larger?
      pipe[i+1] ! next     -- then pass it on
    next > highest         -- larger?
      SEQ
        pipe[i+1] ! highest -- then pass on
                            -- old value and
        highest := next     -- substitute next
```

This does exactly what was described in words above, except for the initial input and final output of a value for highest. It has to be repeated 99 times in each process to pass through all the numbers. Hence:

```
INT highest :
SEQ
  pipe[i] ? highest
  SEQ j = 0 FOR 99
    INT next :
    SEQ
      pipe[i] ? next
      IF
        next <= highest
          pipe[i+1] ! next
        next > highest
          SEQ
            pipe[i+1] ! highest
            highest := next
  pipe[i+1] ! highest
```

Since we know in advance how many times it has to execute, a replicated **SEQ** is preferable to a **WHILE** loop.

This is the whole process which must be executed at each stage of the pipeline, so we can just replicate it, using the index **i**. We can make the program a little tidier at the same time by using abbreviations for **pipe[i]** and **pipe[i+1]**. Note the choice of **j** as the index for the **SEQ** to avoid confusion:

```
PAR i = 0 FOR 100
  input  IS pipe[i] :
  output IS pipe[i+1] :
  INT highest :
  SEQ
    input ? highest
    SEQ j = 0 FOR 99
      INT next :
      SEQ
        input ? next
        IF
          next <= highest
            output ! next
          next > highest
            SEQ
              output ! highest
              highest := next
    output ! highest
```

Although this array of parallel processes does all the necessary work, it isn't yet a whole program. As in the queue example above, we need two extra processes, to run in parallel with our main one, one of which feeds numbers into the pipeline at **pipe[0]**, and another which bleeds the sorted numbers from **pipe[100]**.

These are quite straightforward to write; we'll assume that the numbers to be sorted come from a channel called **input** and that the sorted results go out on a channel called **output**, both of which connect to processes elsewhere in a larger program:

```
SEQ i = 0 FOR 100
  INT unsortednumber :
  SEQ
    input ? unsortednumber
    pipe[0] ! unsortednumber


SEQ i = 0 FOR 100
  INT sortednumber :
  SEQ
    pipe[100] ? sortednumber
    output ! sortednumber
```

The whole program can now be put together. As a finishing gloss we can use an abbreviation for the number of values to be sorted to make it easier to alter:

```
VAL numbers IS 100 :
[numbers+1]CHAN OF INT pipe :
PAR
  PAR i = 0 FOR numbers    -- Set up pipeline
    input  IS pipe[i] :
    output IS pipe[i+1] :
    INT highest :
    SEQ
      input ? highest
      SEQ j = 0 FOR numbers - 1 -- Move data
        INT next :              -- through pipe
        SEQ
          input ? next
          IF
            next <= highest
              output ! next
            next > highest
              SEQ
                output ! highest
                highest := next
      output ! highest

  SEQ i = 0 FOR numbers      -- Feed unsorted
    INT unsortednumber :     -- numbers
    SEQ
      input ? unsortednumber
      pipe[0] ! unsortednumber

  SEQ i = 0 FOR numbers      -- Bleed sorted
    INT sortednumber :       -- numbers
    SEQ
      pipe[numbers] ? sortednumber
      output ! sortednumber
```

The feed, pipeline and bleed processes are combined into a **PAR** so they all run at once. Don't give yourself a headache trying to prove that they all work in sync. This is occam in action; the patient input and output processes guarantee that the three processes will work in harmony.

This program can in fact be made more efficient if we take note of the fact that the end of the number stream comes progressively into sorted order as we move down the pipe. These last, sorted, numbers may be copied straight through without any testing, so that the workload diminishes as they move down the pipe. At process `pipe[i]`, `i` numbers are already in sorted order and `numbers-i` remain unsorted. Hence:

```
PAR i = 0 FOR numbers
  input  IS pipe[i] :
  output IS pipe[i+1] :
  SEQ                            -- sort unsorted
    VAL still.unsorted IS numbers - i :
    INT highest :
    SEQ
      input ? highest
      SEQ j = 0 FOR still.unsorted - 1
        INT next :
        SEQ
          input ? next
          IF
            next <= highest
              output ! next
            next > highest
              SEQ
                output ! highest
                highest := next
      output ! highest
    VAL already.sorted IS i :  -- copy sorted
    SEQ j = 0 FOR already.sorted
      INT pass.on :
      SEQ
        input ? pass.on
        output ! pass.on
```

Hint: It is by no means a trivial exercise to spot those problems which are suitable for this kind of pipelined solution using replicated **PAR**. In general a program which would otherwise be written as two nested loops:

```
WHILE test1
  ...
WHILE test2
  ...
```

is a likely candidate; see if the outer loop can be replaced by a replicated **PAR**. There will be no speed advantage from pipelining unless the inner loop produces a value to pass on early in its execution. If it only produces such a value when it terminates there will be no overlapping, hence no parallelism.

Termination

In this sorting example, the number of values to be sorted is known in advance, so the feed and bleed processes could be programmed with a self terminating replicated **SEQ**.

In programs where indefinite numbers of values are required to pass through a pipeline until told to stop, the feed and bleed processes will need to use **WHILE** loops, and a problem arises about how to stop the pipeline gracefully. This problem is such a general one in concurrent programming that it warrants a chapter to itself; see Chapter 11.

For a pipeline program the best scheme is for the feed process to send a message, through the pipeline itself, which terminates the bleed process and ensures that pipeline is "flushed out" before activity ceases. Merely terminating the feed process on exhaustion of the input stream would cause the pipeline to deadlock while still containing needed results.

Our car production line analogy is again instructive. There are at least two ways to get the workers to knock off for the night; sound a hooter that they can all hear, or tell the first worker in the line "knocking-off time, finish what you're doing then pass it on!".

occam forbids us the "hooter" solution, because it would violate the rule which disallows assignment to shared variables in a **PAR**. The "hooter" would have to be a global variable which gets changed from "go" to "stop"; therefore it could not be legally shared by the components of a **PAR**, and so the message could not be disseminated.

But in any case, the "pass it on" solution is preferable because it leaves the line empty and ready for an orderly shut down.

Replicated ALT

A replicated **ALT** consists of a number of identically structured alternatives each of which is triggered by input from a channel. Like the replicated **PAR**, it is an immensely powerful and significant construct for occam programmers.

As a simple example:

```
[80]CHAN OF INT incoming :
CHAN OF INT outgoing :
PAR
    ...processes feeding incoming channels

    WHILE TRUE
      INT x :
      ALT i = 0 FOR 80
        incoming[i] ? x
            outgoing ! x

    ...process taking from outgoing channel
```

The replicated **ALT** has the effect of an **ALT** with 80 alternatives:

```
ALT
    incoming[0] ? x
      outgoing ! x
    incoming[1] ? x
      outgoing ! x
    incoming[2] ? x
      outgoing ! x
    etc.........
```

What the process does is to monitor the array of channels; every time a value is ready on one of them, it is transferred to the single output channel **outgoing**. The process acts as a multiplexer, merging all communications from the 80 lines down onto a single channel.

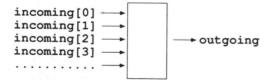

Replicated **ALT** provides an elegant and concise way to build and control switching networks of all shapes and sizes. The array of channels could carry readings from a battery of instruments, or control information from sensors distributed throughout a machine.

Replicated `IF`

The replicated **IF** produces a conditional construct with a number of similarly structured choices.

A simple replicated **IF** such as:

```
IF i = 0 FOR 5
  array[i] = 0
    array[i] := 1
```

would check the first 5 elements of array and replace the first one which was 0 by a 1. If no zeroes were found though it would stop the program; by the nature of the replication process it is not possible to conclude a replicated **IF** with **TRUE SKIP** (unless of course you want an array of **TRUE SKIP**s for some bizarre reason!).

Most uses of replicated **IF** therefore involve nesting it within an outer **IF**. In this case the behaviour if no conditions are met is more appropriate; the next choice in the outer **IF** is considered:

```
IF
  IF i = 0 FOR 5
    array[i] = 0
      array[i] := 1
  TRUE
    SKIP
```

This will now **SKIP** and continue the program if no zeroes are found in array. Such a construct can be used to rewrite the function we defined earlier to find the first occurrence of a character in a string:

```
INT FUNCTION find.char (VAL BYTE char,
                        VAL []BYTE string)
  VAL INT not.found IS -1 :
  INT answer :
  VALOF
    IF
      IF index = 0 FOR SIZE string
        string[index] = char
          answer := index
      TRUE
        answer := not.found
    RESULT answer
  :
```

Note that in this case, the function returns −1 to indicate the character has not been found.

9 Real-time programming in occam

occam concerns itself with the time dimension in a far more profound way than do most conventional languages; the issues of concurrency and synchronisation are tackled in its deep structure. This being so, it is necessary to have ways of measuring and apportioning time in occam programs.

Timers

Timing in occam is provided by declaring named objects of the type **TIMER**. A timer behaves like a channel which can only provide input. The value input from a timer is, not surprisingly, the current time represented as a value of type **INT**.

The simplest kind of timer process would look like this:

```
TIMER clock:
INT time:
clock ? time
```

Technical Note: The "ticks" of this clock will vary from one implementation of occam to another, depending upon the hardware on which it is running. On the INMOS Transputer, the ticks will be in units of (input clock rate)/(5*64) which will normally work out at 64 microseconds per tick; details must be obtained from the hardware manuals for a given system. The time starts from the moment at which the system was switched on, unless the system is provided with a battery backed clock and suitable software to synchronise the occam clock with the real time. Whenever the value of time exceeds the maximum value that can be represented by an **INT** it will become negative and begin to count back towards zero (in accordance with 2's complement signed arithmetic). With a 64 microsecond tick and a 16-bit **INT** this would happen approximately every 4.2 seconds, with a 32-bit **INT** approximately every 76 hours. Time differences must therefore exclusively be calculated using the modulo arithmetic operators, and a long interval can only be timed by breaking it into a series of shorter intervals. Note that one second is exactly 15,625 ticks of 64 microseconds each.

It can be useful to declare more than one timer in a program, even though the value returned from all of them may be the same (if the program is running on a single processor). If there are several independent parallel processes which all require timing, their independence is better expressed if they each have their own timer. For the same reason it may sometimes be useful to declare an array of timers.

Delays

Delays can be added to a program by using a delayed input. This is an input from a timer which cannot proceed until the time reaches a stated value. The operator **AFTER** followed by an expression representing a time is used to cause the delay.

The crude delay procedure we wrote in Chapter 2 can now be replaced by:

```
PROC delay (VAL INT interval)
   TIMER clock :
   INT timenow :
   SEQ
      clock ? timenow
      clock ? AFTER timenow PLUS interval
```

An instance of this procedure, say **delay (6000)**, would pause for **6000** ticks before terminating.

Notice that the delayed input is not an ordinary input process because no variable has its value changed; the value from **clock** is only compared with the value of the expression. Timers are in general rather different from ordinary channels; several components of a **PAR** are allowed to input from the same timer, which would be strictly forbidden for an ordinary channel.

A delayed input could be used in an **ALT** to provide a real- time wait:

```
TIMER clock :
VAL timeout IS 1000 :
INT timenow :
SEQ
  clock ? timenow
  INT x :
  ALT
    input ? x
      ...process
    clock ? AFTER timenow PLUS timeout
      warning ! (17 :: "Timeout on input!")
```

This process will send the timeout warning message if **input** doesn't produce an input within the prescribed time of **1000** ticks.

AFTER can also be used as a comparison operator which returns a truth value; **x AFTER y** is equivalent to **(x MINUS y) > 0**. In other words **AFTER** subtracts **y** from **x**, modulo the largest **INT**, and sees if the result is positive. Modulo arithmetic must always be used for times, hence the use of **PLUS** instead of + in the two examples above. **AFTER** can be used in conditionals to check whether one time is later than another:

```
TIMER clock:
INT proc1.time, proc2.time:
SEQ
  PAR
    SEQ
      ...process 1
      clock ? proc1.time
    SEQ
      ...process 2
      clock ? proc2.time
  IF
    proc1.time AFTER proc2.time
    ...rest of program
```

This provides a check on which of the two parallel processes terminated first.

Take care: When writing programs of this kind it is essential to be aware of the physical details of time representation (see Technical Note above). The test is only meaningful if the difference in the two times is small compared to the largest value represented by an integer. Otherwise a more complex program will be needed.

Priority

So far in this tutorial, the question of priority among processes has been ignored. But when real-time programs are concerned, priority becomes a matter of considerable importance. In the discussion of **ALT** in Chapter 2 for instance, no mention was made of what would happen if two inputs became ready simultaneously. Which process (if any) would be executed?

The answer to that question is "it depends". In an ordinary **ALT**, occam will make an arbitrary choice if the inputs guarding two processes become ready simultaneously. By arbitrary we mean that the outcome is not defined by the language, and may vary from one implementation to another; this does not imply that a random choice will be made, (though that would be one option open to implementors). The crux of the matter is that the programmer cannot predict what will happen in such a case.

In real time programs it will sometimes be necessary to know what will happen in such a case, and so occam allows both **ALT** and **PAR** processes to be prioritised. This is signified by preceding the construct with the word **PRI**.

In both a **PRI ALT** and a **PRI PAR**, the component processes are assigned a priority according to the textual order in which they appear in the program - the first has highest priority and so on.

In a **PRI ALT**, when two inputs become ready simultaneously, the component process with the higher priority will be executed. A special example of the use of a **PRI ALT** is this routine to guarantee that a channel carrying an important signal will be looked at:

```
WHILE cycling
  PRI ALT
    quit ? any
      cycling := false
    TRUE & SKIP
      ...main cycle
```

The **TRUE & SKIP** option is always ready, and if used in an ordinary **ALT** this path could be taken at every cycle without **quit** ever getting a look in. The **PRI ALT** however forces the program to inspect the channel **quit**, because it has a higher priority, and thus guarantees that the cycle can be broken when desired.

In a **PRI PAR**, processes with a lower priority will only be executed if no higher priority process can proceed. So in:

```
PRI PAR
  SEQ
    input1 ? x
    output1 ! x
  SEQ
    input2 ? y
    output2 ! y
```

the second **SEQ** cannot proceed, even when **input2** is ready, unless the first (higher priority) **SEQ** is waiting on its input or output.

PRI PAR can be used in certain real-time applications to service a hardware device sufficiently quickly when the computer has other things to do as well.

```
VAL blocksize IS 1024 :
CHAN OF [blocksize]BYTE nextblock :
PRI PAR
  WHILE TRUE
    [blocksize]BYTE block :
    SEQ
      nextblock ? block
      SEQ i = 0 FOR blocksize
        squirtout ! block[i]
  ...main process
```

In this program, the main process is allowed to proceed only in the slack moments when the device connected to **squirtout** is not being serviced i.e. when waiting to output. Like a spoiled child, the device must always be given full attention when it demands it, so the main process is halted to devote the processor's full power to the **SEQ** loop.

Buffering

If **PRI PAR** is used, the question of buffering may well arise. It is pointless to run a process at high priority to service an impatient device if, whilst servicing that device, it can be kept waiting to communicate with another process.

A high priority process of this kind should have all such communications with other processes buffered, (perhaps using the queuing technique we saw in Chapter 3) so that data can be sent without delay. The size of buffer needed would be tuned to the actual timings of the processes involved.

```
VAL blocksize IS 1024 :
CHAN OF [blocksize]BYTE nextblock :
PRI PAR
  CHAN OF [blocksize]BYTE bufferedblock :
  PAR
    WHILE TRUE                  -- buffer process
      [blocksize]BYTE block :
      SEQ
        nextblock ? block
        bufferedblock ! block
    WHILE TRUE                  -- service process
      [blocksize]BYTE block :
      SEQ
        bufferedblock ? block
        SEQ i = 0 FOR blocksize
          squirtout ! block[i]
...main process
```

In this revised example the input from **nextblock** has a one block buffer added. This reduces the chances of the service routine having to wait to input the next block, which would cause it to delay service to the device. **PRI PAR** should only be used when it is necessary to impose explicit priority and should not be lightly used when an ordinary **PAR** will do.

Glib **Hint**: If you find that you are relying heavily on **PRI PAR**, re-examine your problem carefully; perhaps a differently structured program would work with ordinary **PAR**.

Priority and configuration

Priority has been discussed in this chapter because of its great importance to real time programmers. In formal occam terms it belongs in the next chapter on configuration.

Priority is, strictly speaking, a configuration issue because it does not affect the logical behaviour of a program. Configuration issues are those which allow performance criteria to be met, but which in no way alter the program logic; hence a program can be developed without considering them until the very last stage.

Programs should be developed using ordinary **PAR** and **ALT**, and priority, if it is required, should be left until the logic has been correctly established and the program works.

10 Configuration

Key Idea: Configuration does not affect the logical behaviour of a program. It does enable the program to be arranged so that the performance requirements are met.

Hard channels

Input/output (usually abbreviated to I/O) is the computing term for communication with the outside world. In the case of a computer, the outside world is anything outside of its own CPU and memory space, and it includes mechanical devices such as printers, disk storage, and terminals through which human beings can communicate with the computer.

Readers who have followed this tutorial so far may be forgiven if they have gained the impression that occam lives in a world of Zen-like introspection, contemplating its own inner workings and communicating with itself on a multitude of channels.

If this impression has been given, it was deliberately so. In the attempt to inculcate the general principles of occam, the author has refrained from including anything so far which would tie it to a specific implementation or to specific hardware.

In most computer languages I/O is a problem area. It is always an afterthought, because conventional languages are designed to manipulate data only inside the computer's memory space. As a result I/O tends to be tied to specific hardware devices, and it often violates principles adhered to elsewhere in the language. In occam this is not the case. We could safely ignore I/O until now, because we already know almost all there is to know about it.

occam performs I/O over channels and all we need to know further is how to attach occam channels to real-world hardware devices, which can then be treated just as if they were further occam processes. All the programs that have been developed so far in the tutorial can be made into "real" programs by the addition of a bit of notation tying the abstract channel names to real hardware channels.

In any particular occam implementation there will be a number of I/O channels which can be used by programs. These channels may in some cases lead directly to the hardware, via driver programs which the occam compiler links to your program. In other cases they may lead to the operating system of the host computer, which then handles I/O on behalf of occam.

A typical occam system will support at least channels for a VDU screen, a keyboard, and a filing system. These channels are given numbers which can be found in the manual for the particular occam implementation. Let us suppose that the "hard" channels are numbered as follows:

1 Output to screen

2 Input from keyboard

These numbers are associated with the channel names used in an occam program as follows:

```
PLACE screen   AT 1 :
PLACE keyboard AT 2 :
```

Inside the program these channels can all be input to and output from in the usual fashion. So:

```
VAL message IS "Hello world!" :
SEQ i = 0 FOR SIZE message
  screen ! INT message[i]
```

would display the message on a VDU screen, and:

```
keyboard ? x
```

would input the code for a single character typed at the keyboard into variable **x**.

Take care: A keyboard channel in occam sends the coded value of a single keyboard character to the program. If you press the 1 key, the value received by the program will be not be 1. If the keyboard uses ASCII codes it will be 49, the ASCII code for numeral 1. The same applies in sending characters to the screen; sending 49 will result in a 1 appearing on the screen. Clearly if your program merely receives values from the keyboard and sends them to the screen, then the result will be what is required. But if you wish to do arithmetical calculations with the values, they will have to be adjusted. For instance, when using ASCII codes, you need to subtract 48 from number key values to get the number they represent. Study the example program in Chapter 10 to see how to do numeric output to the screen.

Hardware protocols

Some hardware devices will require various protocols to be adhered to, that is certain special commands and non-data characters may need to be sent (and received) to control the devices, in addition to the actual data.

These are very hardware dependent and cannot be covered in any detail here. But as an example, a screen channel might be buffered, so that characters collect in the buffer before being displayed on the screen. Characters are only displayed when the buffer empties, which happens automatically whenever 80 characters have accumulated, or on demand if the end record code (let's say it's −2) is received. Hence you would need to write:

```
VAL endrecord IS -2 :
...
SEQ
  VAL message IS "Hello world!" :
  SEQ i = 0 FOR SIZE message
    screen ! INT message[i]
  screen ! endrecord
```

to make sure that the message was displayed immediately, as otherwise it would be stored until 68 more characters had been sent.

With file I/O it is certain that some protocol will be required, to open and close files, and to discover the status of filing operations e.g. was the last record successfully written to disk? Again the manual for your particular implementation will elaborate further.

As can be seen, all the example programs we have developed in previous chapters can be quite simply altered to work on a real occam system. We have tended to use the channel names **input** and **output** for channels leading in and out of a program. If these were declared:

```
PLACE input  AT 2 :
PLACE output AT 1 :
```

then the programs could be tested at a terminal with keyboard input. Bear in mind that input only supplies single characters, so a program which requires words to be input will have to collect the characters into an array until a terminating character, usually a carriage return, is received.

Anarchic protocol

Clearly, each channel declared must have a specified protocol as discussed in earlier chapters.

To assist in the cases where a channel protocol is dependent upon the nature of the device with which it communicates, a printer or disk controller for example, occam provides a special protocol. The so-called *anarchic protocol* **ANY**:

```
CHAN OF ANY screen :
```

Practically this declaration specifies a channel which can communicate single objects of any type. So:

```
SEQ
  screen ! 1024
  screen ! 'c'
```

are both valid outputs on the channel screen. The output of the **INT** value **1024** is broken down into its constituent bytes (2 if the machine wordsize is 16-bits, 4 if the machine wordsize is 32-bits), thus the value is output as a stream of bytes.

Ports

In addition to hard channels, occam can address I/O ports as used in conventional computer systems. A port declaration has a data type, e.g.

```
PORT OF BYTE serial1:
```

and the allowed processes are input and output only:

```
serial1 ! 'a'
serial2 ? x
```

This allows ports to be used like channels, rather than like variables, which is more in keeping with the occam style of using channels for all communication and variables for storage.

Ports behave like occam channels in that only one process may input from a port, and only one process may output to a port. Thus ports provide a secure method of accessing external memory mapped status registers etc.

Note that there is no synchronisation mechanism associated with port input and output. Any timing constraints which result from the use of asynchronous external hardware will have to be programmed explicitly. For example, a value read by a port input may depend upon the time at which the input was executed, and inputting at an invalid time would produce unusable data.

During applications development it is recommended that the peripheral is modelled by an occam process connected via channels.

An example of what is required when using such memory mapped devices is this set of occam procedures to drive a UART (Universal Asynchronous Receiver/Transmitter) device:

```
PORT OF BYTE status.reg, data.reg :

PLACE status.reg  AT #3801 :
PLACE data.reg    AT #3803 :

VAL rx.ready IS #01 :      -- first bit mask
VAL tx.ready IS #04 :      -- third bit mask
```

```
PROC delay ()                  -- wait approx 1 msec
  VAL interval IS 1000/64 :
  INT timenow :
  SEQ
    clock ? timenow
    clock ? AFTER timenow PLUS interval
:
PROC poll (INT ready)      -- wait for status
  BYTE status :            -- bit set
  SEQ
    status.reg ? status
    WHILE ((INT status) /\ ready) = 0
      SEQ
        delay ()
        status.reg ? status
:
INT data :
PROC read.data ( )         -- read a character
  BYTE char :
  SEQ
    poll (rx.ready)        -- poll on first bit
    data.reg ? char
    data := (INT char) /\ #7F
:
PROC write.data ( )        -- write a character
  SEQ
    poll (tx.ready)        -- poll on third bit
    data.reg ! BYTE (data /\ #7F)
:
```

This reminds us of the perils of communication programming without the advantages of synchronised channels.

Allocation

occam programs may be designed, written, tested and debugged on a single processor workstation, and then transferred to a network of parallel computers.

The final stage of such a development cycle is to allocate parallel processes in the program to different processors. This allocation is performed by replacing **PAR** with **PLACED PAR** in the appropriate parts of the program. **PLACED PAR** is followed by a placement, which consists of the number of a processor and a process to be run on it.

As an example, the pipelined sorting program we developed in Chapter 3 could be allocated to a linear array of 101 Transputers by the following placement:

```
PLACED PAR
  PLACED PAR i = 0 FOR numbers    -- Pipeline
    PROCESSOR i            -- Allocate processor
      input  IS pipe[i] :
      output IS pipe[i+1] :
      INT highest :
      SEQ
        input ? highest
        SEQ j = 0 FOR numbers-1 -- Move data
          INT next :          -- through pipe
          SEQ
            input ? next
            IF
              next <= highest
                output ! next
              next > highest
                SEQ
                  output ! highest
                  highest := next
        output ! highest
...rest of sort routine
```

The keywords **PLACE** ... **AT** ... allocate a named variable, channel, port or array to a physical memory address. If a program has to store data directly into a range of memory addresses an array could be **PLACE**d at the appropriate range. A typical example of this usage might be to write graphics data into a screen buffer:

```
VAL screenstart IS #B800:
[32000]BYTE screenbuffer:
PLACE screenbuffer AT screenstart:
...
screenbuffer[57] := #FF  -- set all pixels in byte 57
```

This is subject matter beyond the scope of this tutorial but is mentioned here to indicate that these things can be done in occam, without resorting to any lower level of programming.

Summary

None of these operations in any way affect the logic of a program. In other words a program can be developed with little or no thought to such matters and then the required configuration can be performed when the program logic is proven, by text substitutions and additions on a quite minor scale.

It is in this way that occam renders the programming of large and complex arrays of multiple processors manageable, even to the point where much of the programming can be accomplished while the actual hardware is still only a paper design.

11 Terminating concurrent programs

Ensuring the correct termination of programs is a problem inherent in concurrent programming, and one which will be new to programmers whose only experience is in conventional sequential programs. It is a problem faced in all concurrent programs, not merely in occam programs.

In a sequential program there is only a single path, or flow of control through the program when it is running. Even where the program branches, only one branch can be taken at a given time. Therefore, even in a program which is embedded in an outer infinite loop, it is always possible to arrange for control to be "captured" at some point and the program to be stopped.

With concurrent programs employing many parallel processes, this is not the case. If the processes do not communicate with one another, stopping one will leave the others still running. If they do communicate with one another, stopping one may well leave the others deadlocked rather than properly terminated.

Stopping and termination

One mistake which might tempt newcomers to occam is to use **STOP** to try to terminate a program. By its definition **STOP** never terminates. The effect of **STOP** is to start but never proceed. Termination involves completing all the instructions in the program. **STOP** is an instruction which can never be completed.

STOP is useful, as described earlier, to temporarily replace a yet-to-be-written error handler during program development. On a development system, **STOP** may well return you to the editor with a polite message to the effect that your program has stopped.

In a control application though, a stopped program may merely be broken or hung, and the gadget it controlled is no longer under control. If it's a nuclear power station, then this effect of **STOP** should not be recommended. However, the effect of **STOP** is likely to vary between implementations, so check your implementation notes.

Shared variables

Another obvious technique to try, based on sequential programming experience, is to employ a global variable as a flag which is set to "stop" or "go" and is read by all the processes. This is not permitted in occam if the processes are in a **PAR**. Parallel processes are not allowed to share a variable which is changed by assignment or input, for reasons which were explained in Chapter 2.

If it were possible it would not be satisfactory. When the flag is set to "stop", it may not be permissible for all the processes to just quit; the system will be left in a confused state with operations partly finished, and data in wrong places.

Perhaps each process could be allowed to finish what it's doing after it receives the "stop" signal. But then it may require service from another process which has already terminated, and again deadlock results.

There is no solution in this direction. The system has to be considered as a whole, and the shutting down has to be propagated through it in a deliberate manner.

Terminating PAR

Let's take as an example, a pipeline similar to those we developed in Chapter 4 using replicated **PAR**. The pipeline is to process a stream of numbers whose length can only be determined at run time.

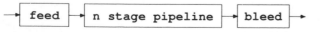

The first thing to make clear is that we must mark the end of the stream. It isn't possible to test for the absence of an input; an absent input simply means deadlock. The last number in the stream must convey the information that there are no more to follow. Let's say that sending a negative number means end of stream.

When the **feed** process receives the end marker, it is not permissible for it to merely terminate:

```
PROC feed ()
  INT x :
  BOOL more :
  SEQ
    more := TRUE
    WHILE more
      SEQ
        input ? x
        IF
          x < 0
            more := FALSE
          x >= 0
            pipe[0] ! x
```

If we do this, the pipeline will stall as its first process, and then all the subsequent ones, deadlock waiting for input from **pipe[0]** that will never come. And the pipeline still contains **n** results which we need to have.

Catching the end marker in **bleed** would be better, as that at least ensures that all the results are out of the pipeline. But it is still not possible to merely terminate **bleed** without deadlocking the rest of the pipe (in this case because **pipe[n]** is waiting for an output that can never proceed).

What's required is the following sequence of events:

1 **feed** detects the end marker and passes it on, then terminates.

2 All the processes in the pipeline do the same.

3 **bleed** simply terminates when it receives the end marker.

In occam this becomes:

```
PROC feed ()
  INT next :
  BOOL more :
  SEQ
    more := TRUE
    WHILE more
      SEQ
        input ? next
        IF
          next < 0
            SEQ
              pipe[0] ! next
              more := FALSE
          next >= 0
            pipe[0] ! next
  :
```

```
PROC bleed ()
  INT next :
  BOOL more :
  SEQ
    more := TRUE
    WHILE more
      SEQ
        pipe[n] ? next
        IF
          next < 0
            more := FALSE
          next >= 0
            output ! next
:

PROC pipeline ()
  PAR i = 0 FOR n
    input  IS pipe[i] :
    output IS pipe[i+1] :
    INT next :
    BOOL more :
    SEQ
      more := TRUE
      WHILE more
        SEQ
          input ? next
          IF
            next < 0
              SEQ
                output ! next
                more := FALSE
            next >= 0
              SEQ
                ...some processing
                output ! next
:

PAR                     -- main process
  feed ()
  pipeline ()
  bleed ()
```

There is an additional assumption here, namely that the process which is connected to the output of **bleed** knows how many numbers were processed, and can terminate itself decently. Perhaps it is the same process that sent the stream to feed, so all's well. If not, it needs either to be told by the process that sent the stream, or we could let the end marker travel one step further.

It isn't possible to give a generally applicable recipe for terminating **PAR** processes; the details will vary from case to case. But there are some general principles illustrated here that can be useful.

1 Correct termination requires knowledge. Processes need to know when to stop.

2 Knowledge requires dissemination. There is no magic telegraph which can let all **PAR** processes know simultaneously.

3 Channels are the proper vehicles for disseminating knowledge to processes. Variables cannot be used to spread knowledge in a **PAR**.

4 There is no place in computer space which is "outside" of a **PAR** process. Control can only come from another component of the **PAR**, via a channel. If you wish to send control signals from the outside world, then there must be a component of the **PAR** which monitors the signal channel.

Terminating ALT

Terminating programs which use **ALT** is quite straightforward, and we have seen an example in the volume controller process in Chapter 2. One of the alternatives of the **ALT** must monitor a signal channel for the quit message:

```
VAL quit IS FALSE :
CHAN OF BOOL signal :
...
BOOL going
SEQ
  going := TRUE
  WHILE going
    INT var1, var2   :
    ALT
      chan1 ? var1
        ...process1
      chan2 ? var2
        ...process2
      signal ? going
        SKIP
```

The problem which can arise here is one of performance alone. The channels in an **ALT** are selected on a first past the post basis, but in the case of a tie they are selected in an arbitrary and implementation dependent fashion. It is not possible therefore to know exactly when a quit command is going to be obeyed; it could be kept out in the cold for an unacceptable length of time by the other alternatives.

The answer, as we saw in the chapter on configuration, is to use a **PRI ALT**, and to assign the highest priority to the alternative monitoring channel **signal**. Now, in the event of a tie, **signal** will always win and the response to a quit command will be predictable.

```
...
PRI ALT
  signal ? going
    SKIP
  chan1 ? var1
    ...process1
  chan2 ? var2
    ...process2
```

12 Occam programming style

Before this tutorial ends it would be as well to look at an example of a larger occam program, and offer some advice on programming style.

The following program is a simple typing tester. It counts the number of words you type, and inserts this number into the text every minute. By inspecting the text when you've finished you can see how many words per minute you achieved in the different sections.

The program is complete and ready to compile on any system whose hardware matches the various allocations made. It should work on any ASCII terminal which uses a buffered screen, though the endrecord character which flushes the buffer may have to be changed (it is often carriage return). One assumption made is that the clock has a low enough tick rate that an **INT** value will not 'wrap around' in less than one minute.

The word counting portion of the program works on the well established principle of distinguishing between being in a word and not in a word, the latter being signalled if the current character is a return, space or tab, none of which are allowed inside words. A new word is detected and counted when **InWord** goes from **FALSE** to **TRUE** as its first character is typed.

```
-- external channels
CHAN OF INT Keyboard :
PLACE Keyboard AT 2 :
CHAN OF INT Screen :
PLACE Screen AT 1 :

-- screen output
VAL Return    IS '*c' (INT) :
VAL Space     IS '*s' (INT) :
VAL Tab       IS '*t' (INT) :
VAL Newline   IS '*n' (INT) :
VAL ControlC  IS  3 :
VAL Bell      IS  7 :
VAL EndRecord IS -2 :

PROC OutputChar (VAL INT Char)
  Screen ! Char
:

PROC FlushScreen ()
  OutputChar (EndRecord)
:

PROC OutputString (VAL []BYTE Message)
  SEQ i = 0 FOR SIZE Message
    Screen ! INT Message[i]
:
```

```
PROC OutputNumber (VAL INT Number)
  VAL Hundreds  IS Number / 100 :
  VAL Rest      IS Number REM 100 :
  VAL Tens      IS Rest / 10 :
  VAL Units     IS Rest REM 10 :
  VAL MakeDigit IS '0' (INT) :
  IF
    Number < 10
      SEQ
        OutputChar (Units + MakeDigit)
        FlushScreen ()
    Number < 100
      SEQ
        OutputChar (Tens + MakeDigit)
        OutputChar (Units + MakeDigit)
        FlushScreen ()
    Number < 1000
      SEQ
        OutputChar (Hundreds + MakeDigit)
        OutputChar (Tens + MakeDigit)
        OutputChar (Units + MakeDigit)
        FlushScreen ()
:

-- time accumulation
TIMER Clock :
VAL TicksPerSecond IS 15625 :
VAL OneMinute      IS 60 * TicksPerSecond :
INT NextMinute, TotalMinutes :

PROC InitTimer ()
  INT TimeNow :
  SEQ
    Clock ? TimeNow
    NextMinute := TimeNow PLUS OneMinute
    TotalMinutes := 0
:

PROC UpdateTimer ()
  SEQ
    NextMinute := NextMinute PLUS OneMinute
    TotalMinutes := TotalMinutes + 1
:

-- word accumulation
INT WordsThisMinute, TotalWords :

PROC InitWordCounts ()
  SEQ
    WordsThisMinute := 0
    TotalWords := 0
:

PROC UpdateWordCounts ()
  SEQ
    TotalWords := TotalWords + WordsThisMinute
    WordsThisMinute := 0
:
```

```
-- statistics
PROC ShowCurrentSpeed ()
  VAL VeryFewWordsPerMinute  IS 5 :
  IF
    WordsThisMinute < VeryFewWordsPerMinute
      SEQ
        OutputChar (Bell)
        OutputString (" [Still awake?] ")
        FlushScreen ()

    WordsThisMinute >= VeryFewWordsPerMinute
      SEQ
        OutputString (" [")
        OutputNumber (WordsThisMinute)
        OutputString (" words/min]")
        FlushScreen ()
:

PROC ShowAverageSpeed ()
  VAL AverageSpeed  IS (TotalWords / TotalMinutes) :
  SEQ
    OutputChar    (Newline)
    OutputString (" You typed ")
    OutputNumber (TotalWords)
    OutputString (" words in ")
    OutputNumber (TotalMinutes)
    OutputString (" minutes.")
    OutputChar    (Newline)
    OutputString (" Average speed = ")
    OutputNumber (AverageSpeed)
    OutputString (" words per minute.")
    FlushScreen ()
:
```

```
BOOL InWord, Active :          -- main process
SEQ
  InitTimer ()
  InitWordCounts ()
  Active      := TRUE
  InWord      := FALSE
  WHILE Active
    INT Char:
    ALT
      NOT InWord & Clock ? AFTER NextMinute
        SEQ
          ShowCurrentSpeed ()
          UpdateWordCounts ()
          UpdateTimer ()
      Keyboard ? Char
        IF
          Char = ControlC
            Active := FALSE
          (Char = Space) OR (Char = Return) OR (Char = Tab)
            SEQ
              InWord := FALSE
              IF
                Char = Return
                  OutputChar (Newline)
                Char <> Return
                  OutputChar (Char)
              FlushScreen ()
          NOT InWord
            SEQ
              InWord := TRUE
              WordsThisMinute := WordsThisMinute + 1
              OutputChar (Char)
              FlushScreen ()
          InWord
            SEQ
              OutputChar (Char)
              FlushScreen ()
  ShowAverageSpeed ()
```

The following points about programming style can be illustrated using this program.

1 The program is factorised to a degree where the amount of code in **PROC**s far exceeds that in the main program loop. For really large occam programs this will typically be even more so, with the great majority of the code being in the **PROC**s.

   The result is a main program which is free from distracting detail, and which is rendered more readable by the high-level **PROC** names from which it is composed. It is also rendered more maintainable, since the body of a **PROC** can be easily changed without affecting the main process, so long as its function remains similar.

2 Abbreviations and declarations are grouped with the **PROC**s which use them, under the functional headings indicated by the comments (eg --**screen output**, --**time accumulation**). Within each functional grouping, declarations of the same sort are kept together, and a consistent order is followed.

   occam does not insist on any particular order for specifications (except that they must immediately precede the process or procedure which is their scope, and with which the colon associates them). It is much easier to find things if you adhere to a consistent order of your choice. Here the order used is:

   channels > timers > abbreviations > variables

3 Use named abbreviations freely. Abbreviations in occam cost nothing, and may improve performance, by allowing the compiler to choose the most efficient implementation. For instance using an abbreviation for an array segment:

```
[1010]INT fred:
SEQ i = 0 FOR 1000
  ...
  WHILE foo > 0
    VAL f IS [fred FROM i FOR 10]:
    SEQ
        ...
```

in an inner loop will yield a worthwhile speed increase because the value of f becomes local to the inner loop process, and because it is recognised by the compiler as a constant and so run-time checks are reduced.

Named constants make a program much more readable; 'magic numbers' peppered throughout a program are hard to understand and even more tedious to alter.

Program readability is not a matter only of aesthetics. A program which you cannot understand two months later is a failure and a waste of time; you will have to repeat most of the mental effort of writing it whenever it needs to be modified or a similar program needs to be written.

4 Choose for yourself a typographic style for names and stick to it. This is a matter of personal preference. One possibility, illustrated in the typist program, is to use initial capitals for separating compound words; others may prefer all lower case and use of the dot (e.g. **show.count**) as used in the remainder of the tutorial.

Use names which are as long as you need to make them meaningful; it costs nothing in program efficiency and it's not worth creating unreadable programs to save a little typing.

5 Keep specifications of all kinds local. Normally they should be placed immediately before the process in which they are used.

Variables are very often used solely as working stores to carry a value from an input process to an output. They can be declared just before the process in which the input and output occur. Only when they need to be free variables (i.e. retain their value) with respect to some loop need they be declared earlier, as in the case of the variables used to accumulate time and word count above.

6 occam lends itself very well to a style of factorisation in which small procedures are written to act as filters. A filter is a program which accepts a stream of inputs, does something to them and sends an equivalent stream of modified outputs.

A larger program is built up by stringing these filters together like beads. If each filter performs a very simple action, enormous flexibility results, as new programs can often be created by a different combination of the same filters.

This technique of programming is well expounded in the classic book "Software Tools" by Kernighan and Plauger, using a form of Fortran (a later edition uses Pascal).

occam is in fact far more suitable for this factorising technique than any conventional language, because channels are natural partners to filters.

occam allows sequences of filters to be connected in parallel, and it provides other models such as the pipeline and the multiplexer that we have seen in this tutorial. Programming can be transformed into a sort of circuit design, connecting filters, switches, pipelines and other "components" using channels as the "wire".

Using such techniques, occam can be employed to describe hardware as well as software systems. If the host processor is the INMOS Transputer, the boundary between the two becomes indistinct, as any occam process describing a hardware device can be implemented by one or more Transputers. Equally, the workings of a Transputer can be described by an occam process.

7 Avoid preoccupation with configuration and priority until the very end of program development. Get the logic of the program working before you consider the real hardware, using "stubs" (small stand-in procedures which more or less emulate the absent device) or **SKIP** and **STOP** where necessary. Configuration can always be performed without altering the logic of the program.

8 Train yourself to look for the inherent parallelism in problems. Parallel programming is in its infancy and there is as yet no large body of knowledge to draw on; you are among the pioneers.

occam was invented to facilitate parallel programming and the potential performance gains it offers. It is relatively easy, if required, to make a parallel algorithm more sequential but making a sequential algorithm more parallel usually involves starting again from scratch. If you write all your programs with **SEQ** you might just as well have used Fortran.

9 Use your occam text very explicitly to guide your design. In a very practical sense, to write an occam program is to write a specification of your problem (which happens to be executable on a computer).

Any occam text whose meaning is not crystal clear should cause you to stop and think again.

The transputer development system

occam compilers provided by INMOS Ltd. are either supplied as standalone compilers or with a programming environment called the Transputer Development System. This environment includes a special editor which has the ability to conceal and reveal text at will by "folding".

The use of this editor has a profound effect upon the way that programs are structured, which is unfortunately rather difficult to convey well on the printed page.

A piece of text may be "folded" down to a single line on the VDU screen. Such lines are marked by a title preceded by three dots ..., just as we have use three dots to hide the detail of processes whose internal structure is not of immediate interest.

Folds may be nested inside other folds to any depth, dividing the program text in a hierarchical or tree-structured manner. A huge program may be folded down to appear as a single line on the screen, and then unfolded progressively and selectively to inspect those parts of the text which need to be edited.

The typing tutor example above has been designed to give some idea of this structure. The comments associated with the various functional groupings (e.g. `...word accumulation`) would each represent a fold in the editor. All the text below such a comment up to the next comment could be folded away, so the fully folded program would look like this:

```
...external channels
...screen output
...time accumulation
...word accumulation
...statistics
...main process
```

If we opened, say, the word accumulation fold, we might find:

```
INT WordsThisMinute, TotalWords :
...PROC InitWordCounts ()
...PROC UpdateWordCounts ()
```

where the bodies of the **PROC**s had themselves been folded away. The effect could be simulated by actually folding the page, concertina fashion, so that the comments line up! In the occam programming system any fold may be opened or closed by moving the screen cursor onto its title and pressing a key.

The implications for program design should be apparent. The unit of occam programming in practice is not the isolated **PROC**, but the fold, which may contain several **PROC**s and their associated abbreviations, variables etc.

The Transputer Development System is supplied with its own user guide and reference manual.

13 Occam 2 language definition

13.1 Introduction

A process starts, performs a number of actions, and then either stops or terminates. Each action may be an assignment, an input or an output. An assignment changes the value of a variable, an input receives a value from a channel, and an output sends a value to a channel.

At any time between its start and termination, a process may be ready to communicate on one or more of its channels. Each channel provides a one way connection between two concurrent processes; one of the processes may only output to the channel, and the other may only input from it.

Communication is synchronised. If a channel is used for input in one process, and output in another, communication takes place when both processes are ready. The inputting and outputting processes then proceed, and the value to be output is copied from the outputting process to the inputting process.

A process may be ready to communicate on any one of a number of channels. Communication takes place when another process is ready to communicate on one of the channels.

13.2 Notation

The following examples illustrate the notation used in the description of occam.

The meaning of

assignment   =   *variable* := *expression*

is "An *assignment* is a *variable* followed by := followed by an *expression*".

The meaning of

action   =   *assignment* | *input* | *output*

is "An *action* is an *assignment* or an *input* or an *output*". This may also be written:

action   =   *assignment*
action   =   *input*
action   =   *output*

The notation { *process* } means "a list of zero or more *processes* on separate lines".

The notation $\{_0$, *expression* } means "a list of zero or more *expressions* separated from each other by , ", and $\{_1$, *expression* } means "a list of one or more *expressions* separated from each other by , ".

Program Format

The format of an occam program is specified by the syntax, and each statement in the program normally occupies a single line. Statements are indented to reflect program structure. Indentation is measured in units of two spaces. Long statements may be broken after an expression operator, , , ; , :=, or the keywords IS, FROM or FOR (and a text string may be broken using a special notation explained below). When a statement is broken, the continuation of the statement on the following line must be indented at least as much as the first line of the statement.

A text string is broken by ending the first line of the string with *, and starting the continuation on the following line with *.

Comments

A comment is introduced by the character pair --. A comment may follow a statement or may occupy a line by itself at the same indentation as the following statement.

13.3   Process

```
process        =        SKIP | STOP
                |   action
                |   construction
                |   instance

action         =        assignment | input | output

construction   =        sequence | conditional | selection | loop
                |   parallel | alternation
```

STOP starts but never proceeds, and never terminates.

SKIP starts, performs no action, and terminates.

```
assignment    =     variable := expression
```

An assignment evaluates the expression and assigns the result to the variable, provided that the type of the variable is that of the expression. Otherwise the assignment is invalid. All other variables are unchanged in value.

```
input   =     channel ? variable
```

An input inputs a value from the channel, assigns it to the variable and then terminates. All other variables are unchanged in value.

```
output   =     channel ! expression
```

An output evaluates the expression, outputs the result to the channel and then terminates.

Sequence

```
sequence   =     SEQ
                    { process }
```

A sequence starts with the start of the first process. Each subsequent process starts if and when its predecessor terminates. The sequence terminates on termination of the last process. A sequence with no component processes behaves like **SKIP**.

Conditional

```
conditional      =     IF
                          { choice }

choice           =     guarded.choice | conditional

guarded.choice   =     boolean
                          process

boolean          =     expression
```

The value of a boolean expression is either true or false. A guarded choice behaves like **STOP** if its boolean is initially false. Otherwise it behaves like **SKIP** and the process, in sequence.

The choices are tested in sequence. The conditional behaves like the first of the choices which can proceed, or like **STOP** if none of them can proceed. A conditional with no component choices behaves like **STOP**.

Case

selection	=	**CASE** *selector*
		{ *option* }

option	=	{$_1$, *expression* }
		process
	|	**ELSE**
		process

selector	=	*expression*

The selector is evaluated, and its value is used to select one of the component options. If the value of the selector is the same as the value of a expression in one of the options, the selection behaves like the process in that option. Otherwise the selection behaves like the process in the **ELSE** option, or like **STOP** if there is no **ELSE** option.

A selection is invalid unless the expressions in all of the options have distinct constant values. A selection must have at most one **ELSE** option.

Loop

loop	=	**WHILE** *boolean*
		process

A loop is defined by

```
WHILE b  =  IF
   P            b
                  SEQ
                    P
                    WHILE b
                      P
                NOT b
                  SKIP
```

Parallel

parallel	=	**PAR**
		{ *process* }

All processes of a parallel start simultaneously, and proceed together. The parallel terminates when all of the processes have terminated. A parallel process is ready to communicate on a channel if any of its components is ready. A parallel with no component processes behaves like **SKIP**.

If a channel is used for input in one process, and output in another, communication takes place when both processes are ready. The inputting and outputting processes then proceed, and the value of the expression specified in the output is assigned to the variable specified in the input.

No variable changed by assignment or input in any of the component processes of a parallel may be used in any other component, no channel may be used for input in more than one component process, and no channel may be used for output in more than one component process. A parallel is invalid unless these non-interference conditions are satisfied.

Alternation

alternation	=	**ALT** { *alternative* }
alternative	=	*guarded.alternative* | *alternation*
guarded.alternative	=	*guard* *process*
guard	=	*input* | *boolean* **&** *input* | *boolean* **&** **SKIP**

A guard behaves like **STOP** if its boolean is initially false, and like the input or **SKIP** otherwise. A guarded alternative behaves like the guard and the process, in sequence.

An alternation behaves like any one of the alternatives which can proceed, and can proceed if any of the alternatives can proceed. An alternation with no component alternatives behaves like **STOP**.

13.4   Replicator

sequence	=	**SEQ** *replicator*
		process
conditional	=	**IF** *replicator*
		choice
parallel	=	**PAR** *replicator*
		process
alternation	=	**ALT** *replicator*
		alternative
replicator	=	*name* = *base* **FOR** *count*
base	=	*expression*
count	=	*expression*

Let *n* be a name, and *B* and *C* be expressions of type **INT** with values *b* and *c*. Let *X* be one of **SEQ**, **PAR**, **ALT** or **IF** and let *Y(n)* be a corresponding process, choice or alternative according to the syntax above. Then

> *X n = B* **FOR** *C*
>   *Y(n)*

specifies the name *n* as a value of type **INT** for use within *Y(n)*.

The meaning of a replicator is defined by

> **SEQ**   *n = B* **FOR** *0* = **SKIP**
>   *Y(n)*

> **IF**   *n = B* **FOR** *0* = **STOP**
>   *Y(n)*

> **PAR**   *n = B* **FOR** *0* = **SKIP**
>   *Y(n)*

> **ALT**   *n = B* **FOR** *0* = **STOP**
>   *Y(n)*

If $c > 0$

> *X n = B* **FOR** *C* = *X*
>   *Y(n)*   *Y(b)*
>   *Y(b+1)*
>   ...
>   *Y(b+c-1)*

If $c < 0$

> *X n = B* **FOR** *C*   is invalid
>   *Y(n)*

13.5   Multiple assignment

| assignment | = | variable.list := expression.list |

| variable.list | = | {₁ , variable } |
| expression.list | = | {₁ , expression } |

A multiple assignment *v1, v2, ... , vn := e1, e2, ... , en* first evaluates in parallel *e1, e2, ... , en* to produce corresponding values *x1, x2, ... , xn* and then behaves like:

```
PAR
  v1 := x1
  v2 := x2
  ...
  vn := xn
```

Notice that the variables *v1, v2, ...* must obey the non-interference conditions of the parallel construct.

13.6   Types

Primitive types

| type | = | primitive.type |
| | | array.type |

primitive.type	=	**CHAN OF** *protocol*
		TIMER
		BOOL
		BYTE
		INT

A communication channel is of type **CHAN OF** *protocol*. Each communication channel enables values to be communicated between two concurrent processes according to the specified *protocol*. A timer is of type **TIMER**. Each timer provides a clock which can be used by any number of concurrent processes. All other primitive types are data types.

Every variable, expression and value has a data type, which defines the interpretation of values of the type.

The values of type **BOOL** are true and false.

The values of type **BYTE** are nonnegative numbers less than *256*.

A value of any integer type is interpreted as a signed integer *n* in the range

$$-(N/2) <= n < (N/2)$$

where *N* is the number of different values which may be represented by variables of the integer type.

INT is the type of signed integer values most efficiently provided by the implementation.

Array types

| array.type | = | [expression] type |

Array types are constructed from component types. An array type is a channel type, timer type or data type, depending on the type of its components. Two arrays have the same type if they have the same number of components and the types of their components are the same.

In the array type [*e*] *T*, the value of *e* defines the number of components in an array of the array type, and *T* defines the type of the components. A component of an array can be selected by a nonnegative value less than the size of the array.

Integer and Real types

$$primitive.type \quad = \quad \begin{array}{l} \textbf{INT16} \\ | \quad \textbf{INT32} \\ | \quad \textbf{INT64} \\ | \quad \textbf{REAL32} \\ | \quad \textbf{REAL64} \end{array}$$

A signed integer value represented in twos complement form using n bits is of type **INTn**. A signed real value is of type **REAL32** or **REAL64**, and is represented according to ANSI/IEEE standard 754-1985.

A value v of type **REAL32** is represented using a sign bit s, an 8 bit exponent e and a 23 bit fraction f. The value v is positive if $s=0$, negative if $s=1$; its magnitude is:

$(2 ** (e-127)) * 1.f$ if $0<e$ and $e<255$
$(2 ** -126) * 0.f$ if $e=0$ and $f<>0$
0 if $e=0$ and $f=0$

Similarly, a value v of type **REAL64** is represented using a sign bit s, an 11 bit exponent e and a 52 bit fraction f. The value v is positive if $s=0$, negative if $s=1$; its magnitude is:

$(2 ** (e-1023)) * 1.f$ if $0<e$ and $e<2047$
$(2 ** -1022) * 0.f$ if $e=0$ and $f<>0$
0 if $e=0$ and $f=0$

Rounding and Truncating

Arithmetic operators with real operands round their results to produce a value of the same type as their operands. Rounding also occurs in explicit type conversions, and in converting real literals into the above representation. Truncation occurs only in explicit type conversions.

It is valid to round a real value v to a value of type T, provided that v differs from some value r of type T by at most one half in the least significant bit position of r. The result is the value of type T nearest to v; if two values of type T are equally near, the one in which the least significant bit is zero is chosen.

Similarly, it is valid to truncate a real value v to a value of type T, provided that v differs from some value t of type T by less than one in the least significant bit position of t. The result is the value of type T nearest to and not larger in magnitude than v.

13.7   Scope

process	=	specification process
choice	=	specification choice
option	=	specification option
alternative	=	specification alternative
specification	=	declaration	abbreviation	definition

A block

    N
    S

behaves like its scope S; the specification N specifies a name, which may be used with this specification only within S.

Let x and y be names, and let $S(x)$ and $S(y)$ be scopes which are similar except that $S(x)$ contains x wherever $S(y)$ contains y, and vice versa. Let $N(x)$ and $N(y)$ be specifications which are similar except that $N(x)$ is a specification of x and $N(y)$ is a specification of y. Then

    N(x) = N(y)
    S(x)   S(y)

Using this rule it is possible to express a process in a canonical form in which no name is specified more than once.

Declaration

    declaration =   type name :

A declaration $T\,x$: declares x as a new channel, variable, timer or array of type T.

A single declaration may declare several names of the same type. Let T be a type and N1, N2, ..., Nn names. Then

    T N1:
    T N2:
    ...   =   T N1, N2, ... , Nn:
    T Nn: P
    P

Abbreviation

    abbreviation =   specifier name IS element :
                   | VAL specifier name IS expression :

An element is either a name, or a subscripted name which selects a component of an array. An abbreviation $S\,n$ IS element : specifies n as an abbreviation for the element. Let e be an element, and $P(e)$ be a process. Then

    S n IS e: =   P(e)
    P(n)

The abbreviation is invalid if *P(n)* contains an assignment or input to a variable in a subscript in *e*.

An abbreviation **VAL** *S n* **IS** *expression* : specifies *n* as an abbreviation for the expression. Let *e* be an expression, and *P(e)* be a process. Then

  VAL *S n* **IS** *e*:   =   *P(e)*
  P(n)

The abbreviation is invalid if *P(n)* contains an assignment or input to a variable in *e*.

  specifier   =   *primitive.type*
          | [] *specifier* | [*expression*] *specifier*

The type of the element or expression in an abbreviation must be compatible with the specifier. A primitive type *T* is compatible with a specifier *T*. A type [*n*] *T* is compatible with a specifier [] *S*, or with a specifier [*n*] *S*, provided that *T* is compatible with *S*.

The specifier can usually be omitted from an abbreviation. Let N be a name, E be an element or expression and S a compatible specifier. Then

  N **IS** E :   =   S N **IS** E :

and

  VAL N **IS** E :   =   **VAL** S N **IS** E :

13.8   Protocol

definition   =   **PROTOCOL** *name* **IS** *simple.protocol* :
                | **PROTOCOL** *name* **IS** *sequential.protocol* :

protocol   =   *name*

Each input or output on a channel must be compatible with the channel protocol named in the declaration of the channel.

A protocol definition specifies the name of a protocol.

Simple protocol

simple.protocol   =   *type*

Let *T* be a data type, *P* a protocol *T* and *c* a channel of type **CHAN OF** *P*. An output *c* ! *e* is compatible with *P* provided that *e* is of type *T*, and an input *c* ? *v* is compatible with *P* provided that *v* is of type *T*.

simple.protocol   =   *type* : : [ ] *type*

input   =   *channel* **?** *input.item*

input.item   =   *variable*
            | *variable* : : *variable*

output   =   *channel* **!** *output.item*

output.item   =   *expression*
            | *expression* : : *expression*

Let *Tn* and *T* be data types, *P* a protocol *Tn* : : [ ] *T*, and *c* a channel of type **CHAN OF** *P*. An output *c* ! *e* : : *a* is compatible with *P* provided that *a* is of type [*n*] *T* and *e* is of type *Tn* ; its effect is to output first *e*, then the first *e* components of *a*. Similarly, an input *c* ? *v* : : *a* is compatible with *P* provided that *a* is of type [*n*] *T* and *v* is of type *Tn*; its effect is to input first *v*, then the first *v* components of *a*.

protocol   =   *simple.protocol*

A simple protocol *P* need not be named; it can be used directly in the channel type **CHAN OF** *P*.

Sequential protocol

sequential.protocol   =   { $_1$; *simple.protocol* }

input   =   *channel* **?** { $_1$; *input.item* }

output   =   *channel* **!** { $_1$; *output.item* }

Let *P* be a protocol *P1; P2; ...; Pn* and *c* be a channel of type **CHAN OF** *P*. The output *c* ! *X1; X2; ...; Xn* is compatible with *P* provided that each *c* ! *Xi* is compatible with the corresponding *Pi*; it outputs *X1, X2, ... , Xn* in sequence.

Similarly, the input *c* ? *X1; X2; ...; Xn* is compatible with *P* provided that each *c* ? *Xi* is compatible with the corresponding *Pi*; it inputs *X1, X2, ... , Xn* in sequence.

Variant protocol

definition	=	**PROTOCOL** *name*
		CASE
		{ *tagged.protocol* }
		:

tagged.protocol	=	*tag*
	|	*tag* ; *protocol*

tag	=	*name*

All of the tags used in a variant protocol must be distinct names. An input or output is compatible with a variant protocol provided that it is compatible with one of the component tagged protocols.

output	=	*channel* **!** *tag*
	|	*channel* **!** *tag* ; {$_1$; *output.item* }

An output c **!** t is compatible with a tagged protocol t.

An output c **!** t; L is compatible with a tagged protocol t; S provided that c **!** L is compatible with S. It first outputs tag t, and then behaves like c **!** L.

case.input	=	*channel* **?** **CASE**
		{ *variant* }

variant	=	*tagged.list*
		process
	|	*specification*
		variant

tagged.list	=	*tag*
	|	*tag* ; {$_1$; *input.item* }

process	=	*case.input*

A case input is compatible with a variant protocol provided that each of its component variants is compatible with some tagged protocol of the variant protocol.

A case input behaves first like an input of a tag t from a channel. The tag is then used to select one of the component variants. If there is a component variant with tagged list t ; L, the list L is input from the channel, and the case then behaves like the associated process. If there is no tagged input with tag t, the case input behaves first like the input of tag t, then like **STOP**.

input	=	*channel* **?** **CASE** *tagged.list*

An input c **?** **CASE** t ; L behaves first like an input of a tag s, and then like an input of L is $s=t$ and like **STOP** otherwise.

alternative	=	*channel* **?** **CASE**
		{ *variant* }
	|	*boolean* **&** *channel* **?** **CASE**
		{ *variant* }

A case input may be used as an alternative in an alternation. It behaves like **STOP** if its boolean is initially false and like the case input otherwise.

13.9   Procedure

definition   =   **PROC** name ({$_0$, formal })
                          body
                       :

formal   =   specifier name
                   | **VAL** specifier name

body   =   process

The definition

  PROC n ({$_0$, formal })
    B
  :

defines n as the name of a procedure.

instance   =   name ({$_0$, actual })

actual   =   element
                   | expression

Let X be a program expressed in the canonical form in which no name is specified more than once. If X contains a procedure definition P (F0, F1, ... , Fn) with body B, then within the scope of P

  P (A0, A1, ... , An)   =   F0 **IS** A0 :
                                 F1 **IS** A1 :

                                 ...
                                 Fn **IS** An :
                                 B

provided that each abbreviation Fi **IS** Ai is valid.

A formal may specify several names. Let S be a *specifier*. Then

  S x1, S x2, ... , S xn   =   S x1, x2, ... , xn

and

  VAL S x1, **VAL** S x2, ... , **VAL** S xn   =   **VAL** S x1, x2, ... , xn

A procedure can always be compiled either by substitution of its body as described above or as a closed subroutine.

13.10   Variable, Channel and Timer

Element

An element has a type, which may be a channel type, timer type or data type. An element of data type also has a value. Elements enable channels, timers, variables or arrays to be selected from arrays.

element   =   element [subscript]
                   | [element **FROM** subscript **FOR** subscript]
                   | name

subscript   =   expression

Let *v* be of type [*n*] *T*, and *e* an expression of type **INT** and value *s*. Then *v*[*e*] is valid only if $0<=s$ and $s<n$; it is the component of *v* selected by *s*.

Let *v* be of type [*n*] *T*. Then [*v* **FROM** *b* **FOR** *c*] is valid only if $c>=0$, $b>=0$ and $(b+c)<=n$; it is an array of type [*c*] *T* with components *v*[*b*], *v*[*b+1*], ... *v*[*(b+c)-1*].

The type of an element consisting of a name is that of the name.

Variable

> *variable*   =   *element*

Every variable has a value which may be changed by assignment or input. The value of a variable is the value most recently assigned to it, or is arbitrary if no value has been assigned to it. An assignment or input is invalid unless the type of the variable is that of the value assigned.

Let *v* be a variable of type [*n*] *T*, and *e* an expression of type *T*. If $0<=s$ and $s<n$, then *v*[*s*] := *e* assigns to *v* a new value in which the value of the component selected by *s* is replaced by the value of *e*, and all other components are unchanged. Otherwise the assignment is invalid.

Let *v* be a variable of type [*n*] *T*. Let *s* be [*v* **FROM** *b* **FOR** *c*] and *e* an expression of the same type as *s*, [*c*] *T*. The assignment *s* := *e* assigns to each component of *s* the corresponding component of *e*, provided that no component of *e* is also a component of *s*. Otherwise *s* := *e* is invalid.

Let *x* be a channel, *s* be [*v* **FROM** *b* **FOR** *c*], *e* an expression. The combined effect of *x*?*s* and *x*!*e* is *s* := *e*.

Channel and Timer

> *channel*   =   *element*

> *timer*   =   *element*

A channel element used for input or output is invalid unless it is of type **CHAN OF** *protocol*. A timer element used for timer input or delayed input is invalid unless it is of type **TIMER**.

13.11   Literal

A literal has a data type and a value.

> | *literal* | = | *integer* |
> |---|---|---|
> | | \| | *byte* |
> | | \| | *integer*(*type*) |
> | | \| | *byte*(*type*) |
> | | \| | *real*(*type*) |
> | | \| | *string* |
> | | \| | **TRUE** \| **FALSE** |

> *integer*   =   *digits* \| #*digits*

> *byte*   =   ' *character*'

> *real*   =   *digits*. *digits* \| *digits*. *digits***E***exponent*

> *exponent*   =   +*digits* \| −*digits*

An integer literal is a decimal number, or # followed by a hexadecimal number. A byte literal is an ASCII character enclosed in single quotation marks: '.

An integer literal is of type **INT**, and a byte literal is of type **BYTE**. Let x be an integer or byte literal, and T be **BYTE** or an integer type. A literal $x(T)$ is a value of type T and value x, provided that x can be exactly represented as a value of type T. Otherwise $x(T)$ is invalid.

Let T be a real type. The value of the literal $f(T)$ is f rounded to a value of type T, and the value of the literal $fEe(T)$ is $f * (10 ** e)$ rounded to a value of type T.

A string is represented as a sequence of ASCII characters, enclosed by double quotation marks: ". Let s be a string of n characters. The value of s is an array of type $[n]$ **BYTE**; the value of each component of the array is the value of the corresponding ASCII character of the string.

The literals **TRUE** and **FALSE** represent the Boolean values true and false respectively.

13.12   Expression

An expression has a data type and a value. Expressions are constructed from operands, operators and parentheses.

```
operand    =      element
           |      literal
           |      table
           |      (expression)
```

The value of an operand is that of an element, literal, table or expression.

```
table    =      table [ subscript ]
         |      [ {₁ , expression } ]
         |      [ table FROM subscript FOR count ]
```

The value of $[e1, e2, ..., en]$ is an array in which each component has the value and type of the corresponding expression.

```
expression    =      monadic.operator operand
              |      operand dyadic.operator operand
              |      conversion
              |      operand
```

The arithmetic operators **+**, **-**, *****, **/**, **REM** yield the arithmetic sum, difference, product, quotient and remainder, respectively. Both operands of an arithmetic operator must be of the same integer or real type, and the result is of the same type as the operands. The arithmetic operators treat integer operands as signed integer values, and produce signed integer results. The type of $-x$ is that of x, and its value is $(0 - x)$.

Let m and n be integers. The result of m / n is rounded towards zero, being positive if both m and n are of the same sign, negative otherwise. The result of m **REM** n is the remainder of m / n, and its sign is the same as the sign of m. Regardless of the signs of m and n and provided that n is nonzero

$$m = ((n * (m/n)) + (m \text{ REM } n))$$

The result of a real arithmetic expression e of type T is the value of e, rounded to the nearest value of type T. If x and y are real, the result r of x **REM** y is $x - (y * n)$, where n is the result of x / y rounded to the nearest integer value; **REM** can therefore yield a negative value.

The operators **+**, **-**, *****, **/**, **REM** are invalid if the result cannot be represented as a value of the same type as the operands.

Both operands of the modulo operators **PLUS**, **MINUS** and **TIMES** must be of the same integer type, and the result is of the same type as the operands. Let N be the number of different values which may be represented using the type of the expression. The modulo operators obey the following rules:

$(i$ **PLUS** $j) = (i + j) + (k * N)$

where k is the unique integer for which

$(i + j) + (k * N) >= -(N/2)$ and
$(i + j) + (k * N) < (N/2)$

Similarly:

$(i$ **MINUS** $j) = (i - j) + k * N$
$(i$ **TIMES** $j) = (i * j) + k * N$

The operator **AFTER** is defined by:

$(i$ **AFTER** $j) = (i$ **MINUS** $j)$ $\$>\$$ 0

The bitwise operators $/\backslash$, $\backslash/$, $><$ yield the bitwise and, or and exclusive or of their operands. Both operands must be of the same integer type, and the result is of the same type as the operands. Each bit of the result is produced from the corresponding bits of the operands according to the following rules:

$b >< 0 = b$ $0 >< 1 = 1$ $1 >< 1 = 0$
$b /\backslash 0 = 0$ $b /\backslash 1 = b$
$b \backslash/ 0 = b$ $b \backslash/ 1 = 1$

where b is 0 or 1.

The bitwise operator $\sim$ yields the bitwise not of its operand, which must be of integer type. Each bit of the result is produced from the operand as follows:

$\sim 1 = 0$ $\sim 0 = 1$

In a shift expression $n << c$ or $n >> c$, n and the result are of the same integer type, and c is of type **INT**. The shift operators yield results according to the following rules:

$n << 1 = n$ **PLUS** n
$n >> 1 = m$, where $m >= 0$ and $((m<<1)+(n /\backslash 1)) = n$

Let O be $<<$ or $>>$, and let b be the number of bits needed to represent a value of type n. Then

$(n$ O $0) = n$
if $c < 0$ or $c > b$ n O c is invalid
if $c > 0$ n O $c = (n$ O $1)$ O $(c-1)$

The boolean operators **NOT**, **AND**, **OR** yield boolean results according to the following rules:

NOT *false* = *true*   **NOT** *true* = *false*
false **AND** *b* = *false*   *true* **AND** *b* = *b*
false **OR** *b* = *b*   *true* **OR** *b* = *true*

where b is a boolean value.

Let O be one of the operators **AND**, **OR**.

e1 O e2 O ... O en   =   (e1 O (e2 O (... O en) ...))

The relational operators =, <>, <, <=, >, >= yield a result of type **BOOL**. The operands of = and <> must be of the same primitive data type. The operands of <, <=, >, >= must be of the same integer, byte or real type. The result of $x = y$ is true if the value of x is equal to that of y. The result of $x < y$ is true if the numerical value of x is strictly less than that of y. The other operators obey the following rules:

$(x <> y) = $ **NOT** $(x = y)$ $(x >= y) = $ **NOT** $(x < y)$
$(x > y) = (y < x)$ $(x <= y) = $ **NOT** $(x > y)$

where x and y are any values.

The operand of the monadic operator **SIZE** must be an array type. Let x be of type $[n]$ T. The expression **SIZE** x is of type **INT**; its value is n.

expression   =   **MOSTPOS** type | **MOSTNEG** type

Let I be an integer type, and N be the number of values representable using type I. The type of **MOSTPOS** I is I; its value is $(N/2)-1$. Similarly, the type of **MOSTNEG** I is I; its value is $-(N/2)$.

conversion   =   type operand
             | type **ROUND** operand
             | type **TRUNC** operand

The type of a conversion T e, T **ROUND** e or T **TRUNC** e is T; its value is the value of e converted to a value of type T. Both T and the type of e must be primitive types.

Let e be an expression of value v, and of integer or **BYTE** type. Then **BOOL** e is invalid unless $v=0$ or $v=1$; its value is **TRUE** if $v=1$, **FALSE** if $v=0$. Let T be any integer type, **BYTE** or **BOOL**. Then T **TRUE**$=1$ and T **FALSE**$=0$.

Let e be an expression of value v, and of integer or **BYTE** type. Let I be an integer type and N the number of values representable in type I. The value of I e is v, provided that $-(N/2) <= v < (N/2)$. The value of **BYTE** e is v, provided that $0 <= v < 256$.

Let e be an expression of value v and of integer type. Let R be a real type. The value of R **ROUND** e is the value of e rounded to a value of type R, and the the value of R **TRUNC** e is the value of e truncated to a value of type R. R e is invalid.

Let e be an expression of value v, and of real type S. Let R be a real type. Then R e is valid if every value of type S is exactly representable as a value of type R, and its value is v.

Let e be an expression of value v and of real type. Let T be an integer or real type. The result of T **ROUND** e is the value of e rounded to a value of type T, and the result of T **TRUNC** e is the value of e truncated to a value of type T.

13.13   Function

Value processes

value.process	=	*valof*
valof	=	**VALOF**
		process
		RESULT *expression.list*

valof	=	specification
		valof

The valof

```
VALOF
  P
  RESULT E
```

first executes process P, and then evaluates the expression list E to produce a list of result values.

operand	=	(*value.process*
		)
expression list	=	(*value.process*
		)

A value process with a single result value may be used as an expression operand, and a value process with one or more result values may be used as an expression list in a multiple assignment.

A value process may not contain parallel or alternative constructs and may not contain inputs or outputs. Any assignment in a value process must be to a variable declared within the value process.

Function definition

definition	=	$\{_1$, *primitive.type* $\}$ **FUNCTION** *name* ($\{_0$, *formal* $\}$)
		function.body
		:
function.body	=	*value.process*

The definition

$$\{_1 \text{ , } \textit{primitive.type} \} \textbf{ FUNCTION } n \text{ (} \{_0 \text{ , } \textit{formal} \} \text{)}$$
```
    B
  :
```

defines *n* as the name of a function with a body B which computes one or more values with types specified by the list preceding **FUNCTION**. Each formal in the function definition must have the form **VAL** *S n*.

operand	=	*name* ($\{_0$, *expression* $\}$)
expression list	=	*name* ($\{_0$, *expression* $\}$)

Let *X* be a program expressed in the canonical form in which no name is specified more than once. If *X* contains a function definition *T1*, *T2*, ..., *Tn* F (*F0*, *F1*, ... , *Fn*) with body *B*, then within the scope of *F*

$$F \ (\ E0, \ E1, \ \dots \ , \ En \ ) \quad = \quad (\quad F0 \ \textbf{IS} \ E0 \ :$$
$$F1 \ \textbf{IS} \ E1 \ :$$
$$\dots$$
$$Fn \ \textbf{IS} \ En \ :$$
$$B$$
$$)$$

provided that each abbreviation *Fi* **IS** *Ei* is valid.

definition = {$_1$, *primitive.type* } **FUNCTION** *name* ({$_0$, *formal* }) **IS** *expression.list* :

An expression list may be used as a function body in place of a value process. The meaning of

{$_1$, *primitive.type* } **FUNCTION** *name* ({$_0$, *formal* }) **IS** *expression.list* :

is the same as that of

{$_1$, *primitive.type* } **FUNCTION** *name* ({$_0$, *formal* })
  VALOF
    SKIP
    RESULT expression.list
:

A function can always be compiled either by substitution of its body as described above or as a closed subroutine.

13.14   Timer input

input =   *timer.input*
    | *delayed.input*

timer.input =   *timer* ? *variable*

A timer input sets the variable to a value of type **INT** representing the time. The value is derived from a clock, which changes at regular intervals. The successive values of the clock are produced by:

clock := *clock* **PLUS** *1*

delayed.input =   *timer* ? **AFTER** *expression*

A delayed input is unable to proceed until the value of the clock satisfies *(clock* **AFTER** *e)*, where *e* is the value of the expression.

13.15   Character set

The occam characters are:

Alphabetic characters

```
ABCDEFGHIJKLMNOPQRSTUVWXYZ
abcdefghijklmnopqrstuvwxyz
```

Digits

```
0123456789
```

Special characters

```
!"#&'()*+,-./:;<=>?[]
```

The space character

Strings and character constants may contain any occam character (except *, ' and "). Certain characters are represented as follows:

*c	*C	carriage return
*n	*N	newline
*t	*T	horizontal tabulate
*s	*S	space
*'		quotation mark
*"		double quotation mark
**		asterisk

Any character can be represented by *# followed by two hexadecimal digits.

A name consists of a sequence of alphabetic characters, decimal digits and dots (.), the first of which must be an alphabetic character. Two names are the same only if they consist of the same sequence of characters and corresponding characters have the same case.

Other characters

An implementation may provide other characters for use in strings and character constants.

An implementation may also provide the following equivalences

```
REM      =   \
BITAND   =   /\
BITOR    =   \/
BITNOT   =   ~
$        =   #
```

13.16   Configuration

Configuration does not affect the logical behaviour of a program. However, it does enable the program to be arranged to ensure that performance requirements are met.

placedpar   =   **PLACED PAR**
                     { *placedpar* }
                  | **PLACED PAR** *replicator*
                     placedpar
                  | **PROCESSOR** *expression*
                     process

parallel   =   *placedpar*

Each process in a placedpar is executed by a separate processor. Let *e* be an expression, and *P* be a process. The placedpar

   PROCESSOR *e*
      P

executes the process *P* on processor *e*. Where the value of *e* is the number of the processor to execute the component process. The variables and timers used in each component process of a placedpar must be declared within the component process.

parallel   =   **PRI PAR**
                     { *process* }
                  | **PRI PAR** *replicator*
                     process

Each process is executed at a separate priority. The first process is the highest priority, the last the lowest. If *P* and *Q* are two concurrent processes with priorities *p* and *q* such that $p < q$, then *Q* is only allowed to proceed when *P* cannot proceed.

alternation   =   **PRI ALT**
                        { *alternative* }
                     | **PRI ALT** *replicator*
                        alternative

If several alternatives can proceed, the alternation behaves like the first in textual sequence.

process   =   *allocation*
                  process

allocation   =   **PLACE** *name* **AT** *expression* :

An allocation **PLACE** *n* **AT** *e* : allocates the variable, channel, timer or array *n* to *address e*.

13.17   Invalid processes

Invalid processes which are not detected by the compiler can behave in one of the following three ways:

Cause the process to **STOP** allowing other processes to continue.

Cause the whole system to halt.

Have an arbitrary (undefined) effect.

A process containing an invalid expression is treated in the same way as an invalid process.

13.18   Retyping

definition   =   *specifier name* **RETYPES** *element* :
              | **VAL** *specifier name* **RETYPES** *expression* :

An implementation of occam will normally represent variables using a number of bytes or words in a computer memory. It is sometimes possible to interpret this representation as a variable or value of a different type.

The definition T n **RETYPES** e : specifies n as an element of type T, and [ ] T n **RETYPES** e : specifies n as an element of type [x] T. The definition S n **RETYPES** e : is invalid if the scope of n contains an assignment or input to a variable in a subscript in e.

The definition **VAL** T n **RETYPES** e : specifies n as an expression of type T, and **VAL** [ ] T n **RETYPES** e : specifies n as an expression of type [x] T. The definition **VAL** S n **RETYPES** e : is invalid if the scope of n contains an assignment or input to a variable in e.

The use of the retyping conversion will normally result in implementation dependent processes, as the representation of variables will vary from one implementation to another.

13.19   External input and output

Memory mapped interfaces

type   =   **PORT OF** *type*

port   =   *element*

A process may communicate with external devices which are connected to the processor's memory system. A port specification is similar to a channel specification, and the type used in a port specification must be a data type.

input   =   *port* ? *variable*

output   =   *port* ! *expression*

A port input inputs a value from the port, assigns it to the variable and then terminates. A port output evaluates the expression and outputs the result to the port. A program is invalid if any port is used for input or output in more than one component of a parallel.

Channels without protocol

protocol   =   **ANY**

Let c be a channel with type **CHAN OF ANY**. Then c may be used to input or output values of data type. Let e be an expression of type T. Let x be defined by

   VAL [ ] **BYTE** x **RETYPES** e :

Then the meaning of c ! e is that of c ! x. Similarly, let v be an expression of type T. Let x be defined by

   [ ] **BYTE** x **RETYPES** v :

Then the meaning of c ? v is that of c ? x.

13.20   Usage rules check list

This section summarises the rules which govern the use of variables, channels, timers, ports and arrays in parallel constructions, and the rules which govern abbreviations and parameters.

Usage in parallel

The purpose of these rules is to prevent parallel processes from sharing variables, to ensure that each channel connects only two parallel processes, and to ensure that the connection of channels is unidirectional. The rules allow most of the checking for valid usage to be performed by a compiler, thus reducing runtime overheads.

- A channel implements a point-to-point communication between two parallel processes. The name of a channel may only be used in one component of a parallel for input, and in one other component of the parallel for output.

- A timer may be used for input by any number of components of a parallel.

- A variable or component of an array of variables, which is assigned to in a component of a parallel, may not appear in any other component of the parallel.

- An array may be used in more than one component of a parallel, if and only if the subscripts used to select components of the array can be determined at compile time. Otherwise the array may only be used in one component of the parallel.

- Several abbreviations can decompose an array into non-overlapping disjoint parts; components of these parts may then be selected using variable subscripts.

- A port may be used in only one component of a parallel.

The rules for abbreviations

The purpose of these rules is to ensure that each name identifies a unique object, and that the substitution semantics are maintained.

- All reference to an abbreviated element must be via the abbreviation only, with the exception that array elements may be further abbreviated providing the later abbreviations do not include components of the array already abbreviated.

- Variables used in an abbreviated expression may not be assigned to by input or assignment within the scope of the abbreviation.

- The abbreviated expression must be valid, i.e. in range and not subject to overflow, and all subscript expressions must be in range.

- All subscript expressions used in an element abbreviation must be valid, i.e. not subject to overflow and in range.

- All reference to a *retyped* element must be via the new name only, with the exception that array elements may be further retyped providing the later retyping conversions do not include components of the array already retyped.

- Variables used in a retyping conversion may not be assigned to by input or assignment within the scope of the new name.

The rules for procedures

- The rules for procedure parameters follow from those for abbreviations, but in addition a channel parameter or free channel may not be used for both input or output in a procedure.

The rules for value processes and functions

- Functions may only have value parameters.

- Only variables declared within the scope of a value process may be assigned to. Free names may be used in expressions.

- A value process may not contain inputs, outputs, parallels or alternations.

- The body of a procedure used within a function must also obey these rules.

Index

Abbreviation 32, 41, 94, 108
  rules **108**
Allocation 72
Alternation 90
Alternative processes 26
Anarchic protocol 70
Arithmetic 30
Arrays 39, 108
Array protocol 46
Array segments 40
Array types 40, 92
Assignment processes 13

Bit operators 31
Boolean type 18
Buffering 67

Case 89
Case Input 48
Channel 11, 12, 98, 99, 108
Channel type and protocol 18
Channels without protocol 107
Character set 105
Characters and strings 18
Checking usage 108
Comments 88
Communicating processes 21
Communication 14
Concurrency 7, 8
Concurrent programming 7
Concurrent systems 3
Conditional 88
Conditional processes 24
Configuration 68, 106
Constants 18
Constructions 15

Data types 17
Deadlock 23
Declaration 94

Element 98
Expression 100
External input and output 107

Functions 36, 103, 109
Function definition 103

Hard channels 69
Hardware protocols 70

INMOS 3, 37, 65, 83, 84
Input process 13
Integer types 93
Invalid processes 106

Known Input 49

Language definition 3
Literal 99
Loop 89

Memory mapped interface 107
Modelling 7
Multidimensional arrays 42
Multiple assignment 92

Names 17
Naming protocols 45
Notation 87

Output process 14

PAR construction 16
Parallel 89, 106, 108
Parallel computer systems 3
Parallel processing 8
Parameters 34
Parameter passing 35
Pipelined processing 58
PLACED PAR 106
Ports 71, 108
Primitive processes 13
Priority 66, 68
Procedures 32, 98, 108
Process 88
Processes and channels 10
PROCESSOR 106
Program format 87
Protocol 96

Real types 93
Real world model 7
Repetitive processes 23
Replicated ALT 63
Replicated IF 64
Replicated PAR 56
Replicated SEQ 55
Replicator 91, 106
Retyping 107
Rounding 93

Scope 19, 94
Selection processes 26
SEQ construction 15
Sequence 88
Sequential protocol 46, 96
Shared variables 21, 75
Simple protocol 45, 96
SKIP and STOP 14
Sort program 59
Stopping and termination 75

String output   52
Subscript   108
Synchronisation   8

Tables   41
Tag-Only types   49
Terminating ALT   78
Terminating PAR   75
Termination   62
Termination and stopping   15
Timers   65, 98, 99, 108
Timer input   104
Timer type   18
Transputer   3, 65, 83
Transputer Development System   84
Truncating   93
Type conversions   31
Types   92
  specifications and scope   17

Usage rules   108

Value process   109
Value processes   103
Variable   98, 99, 108
Variant protocol   47, 97